CREATE A SUCCESSFUL WEBSITE

CREATE A SUCCESSFUL WEBSITE

PAULA WYNNE

First Published in Great Britain 2010 by
Lean Marketing Press (www.leanmarketingpress.com)

© Copyright Paula Wynne

Author photo on jacket by Sue Reeves (www.suepix.co.uk)

"Fear can keep you prisoner.
Hope can set you free."
Andy DuFrane, Shawshank Redemption

Contents

Praise

"Wow! This incredible no-nonsense guide, *Create a Successful Website*, takes you through all the steps in setting up an online business: from research and planning, to branding and content with e-commerce and revenue earning options. A must read!"

Caroline Marsh, star of C4's Secret Millionaire

"As an analogue entrepreneur in a digital age I'm fascinated by any book which can simplify the Internet - and more importantly how to make money from it. Having been exploited by some costly website developers in the past I'd highly recommend Paula's book as a way of empowering you to create your own site at a fraction of the cost."

**Rachel Elnaugh, entrepreneur and star of BBC TV's
Dragon's Den www.rachelelnaugh.com**

"My advice is that you must read this book cover to cover, before you even think about or attempt to create a website! It is rare to find someone who can combine technical language with business needs and common sense. The highlighted top tips from experts are brilliant as it's invaluable to get a different perspective from a range of industries – and you know these people have been there and done it successfully. This definitely gives the book a Wow Factor! Whether you need to start a website from scratch or brush up and tweak an existing site - read the book from cover to cover. There is something in it for everyone - from a simple hobby site, an online presence right up to a full throttle internet business."

Claire Young, Finalist in BBC TV's The Apprentice

"Paula Wynne's book, *Create a Successful Website*, is what small businesses need if they cannot afford a professional designer to do their website for them - and very few can. Good designers don't come cheap, but good design is vital. Her DIY approach could be the solution."

**Prue Leith, author of Choral Society,
The Gardener, Leaving Patrick and Sisters**

"A must-read for anyone who wants to get on with an internet business."

Anne Diamond, Journalist, Broadcaster and Health Campaigner

"This book will fly! I read it in one sitting and learnt so much. What I love about *Create a Successful Website* is that it feels like you've got a friendly, clever, web-savvy mate just chatting you through the techie, hard bits of setting up a website and creating an online business. It's so clear and easy to understand. Paula has thought of everything, and the fact that she's been through the process the hard way, researching and creating her own websites herself, really shows.

"I'm in the process of setting up two websites, and there are so many things I didn't even know existed until I read the book. She's done the hard work for us. It's an absolute must-read for anyone new to this, I can't think of a better start for your website business."

Fiona Wright, freelance journalist, features writer Woman and Home, co-founder of TestDriveAnyJob.com and JuniorLife.co.uk

"Clear, easy-to-follow screen shots and instructions will guide you through each task from beginning to end."

Julie Hearn, author of Rowan The Strange, Carnegie Medal Shortlist for 2010

"Crammed with useful, proven and easy to implement tips, *Create a Successful Website* will be an indispensable asset on any business bookshelf. Paula has an engaging, friendly and accessible style and she writes from a position of knowledge that has quite clearly been acquired and honed over many years. Forget the complex and the theoretical; this is all about implementation and Paula makes it incredibly straightforward. What also gives this book the X factor is the stellar line up of excellent contributors, each one an expert within their own field. In the current economic climate, the need for good business books is greater than ever. Empowerment is all. *Create a Successful Website* really does deliver."

Dee Blick FCIM, Financial Mail Marketing Columnist, BT blogger and author of Powerful Marketing on a Shoestring Budget for Small Businesses

"*Create a Successful Website* is a book which proves that anyone with a passion in life can benefit hugely from owning a website to promote their interests. If you are thinking of setting up a web business, or even just a profitable blog or similar, this book sees you through from A-Z."

Elisa Roche, Showbusiness Editor, The Daily Express

"As an IT novice and a technophobe, Paula's book, *Create a Successful Website*, is written with the likes of me in mind. Without a web site now you really can't be taken seriously in business so this book will help you get there - the helping hand of a virtual professional!"
Jo Haigh, Bestselling Author of The Business Rules, An Entrepreneur's Guide, and Tales from the Glass Ceiling - A Survival Guide for Women in Business

"Want to get started with an online business? Read Paula Wynne's *Create a Successful Website* - it's the best start up you can read."
Korky Paul, Illustrator of Winnie the Witch amongst many others

"Paula's guide to setting up your own website makes the process straightforward and understandable. It's highly readable, even for the least techie person, and includes useful tips from other business people who have already gone down the same path. It's ideal if you're working from home and want a web presence without the expense of taking on a designer, or would like to understand what your designer is talking about!"
Judy Heminsley, author of Work from Home Wisdom

"Anyone setting out to explore and conquer the web needs a practical step by step guide. Well here it is!"
Clem Chambers, CEO of ADVFN.com and author of The Armageddon Trade and The Twain Maxim

"What a great read! An easy to follow guide to creating a successful website and achieving an online presence. Paula's writing style keeps you wanting to read more."
Lisa Ibbotson, Director and Founder of Women on Their Way

"What a fantastic, straightforward and honest book. I'll be recommending it to anyone wanting to get started with creating a successful website."
Jackie Brennan, Founder of FreshIdeas Events

"Learning how to create a website can be an exhausting task; following this step-by-step guide will most definitely help you succeed."
Debbie Bird, Editor of Babyworld

"*Create A Successful Website* is a very intelligent book, well crafted and easy to understand. The depth of content is outstanding; this is a one stop shop for knowledge."
Paul Handley, Iconic Gifts, www.iconicgifts.com

Acknowledgements

Thank you for picking up this book and I hope you enjoy reading it. By the end, you will have a fantastic blueprint for your website, from preparation and planning, to branding and choosing a website right through to e-commerce and revenue earning.

Firstly, I want to thank Debbie Jenkins and Joe Gregory from Lean Marketing Press for believing in my proposal and giving me the chance to bring my book to life. Also, thanks to the team at Secure Trading (www.securetrading.com) for reading the E-commerce section and checking all the facts.

I would like to say an extra special thanks to all the experts who have given up their time to offer you their best advice in setting up an online business.

- Jo Haigh
- Karen Hanton
- Richard Alvin
- Polly Gowers

- Max Benson, MBE
- Carrie Longton
- Debbie Bird
- Clare Medden

Special Thanks

I would like to mention some of the special people in my life who have always supported my dream to become an author!

My Partner, Ken: you're a constant source of words, wit, smiles, laughter and strength.

My Son, Kent: you have lived through my dream and I encourage you and Jane, Jack, Caydon, Cameron and Tanna and all your cousins to pursue your dreams with every ounce of energy and to always reach for the sky.

My Mom: you have always believed in me, a Mother's love sustains, builds and grows.

Three people who are no longer with me, but I know they look down proudly: Penrose, Granny and Daddy.

For my brothers and sisters and everyone in my family: for every dream we've ever dared to dream.

Foreword

My advice is that you must read this book cover to cover, before you even think about or attempt to create a website!

Being a passionate entrepreneur myself I know of the temptation to dive off into a frenzy of creativity, plans and urgency to get online, but mistakes can easily happen – costing precious time and money.

Since appearing on the BBC1 series The Apprentice I've set up four successful websites and learnt key lessons along the way. I wish I'd discovered Paula's wisdom beforehand; I would have saved myself crucial start up budget.

Even though I consider myself slightly young and hip (I am a cool 31 years old) technically I'm useless. There are countless gadgets and endless jargon that I don't understand. As a commercial person it frustrates me not to understand everything. Unfortunately, when it comes to web design and programme structure, I'm at a loss. This leaves one in a vulnerable position. It is easy for folks to sell you an 'all singing all dancing wizzie website' which costs you big bucks – when actually you may be able to do it all for free or a fraction of the cost, as shown in this book.

It is rare to find someone who can combine technical language with business needs and common sense. This book could be called "Help, I need a website" and will answer all your start up questions before you plunge into the unknown.

Aside from good straight forward guidance and online knowledge this book is an ideal step-by-step plan. It will make you think about your brand and take small steps to being a big player one day.

The highlighted top tips from experts are brilliant as it's invaluable to get a different perspective from a range of industries – and you know these people have been there and done it successfully. Just think of the resource you will have with the knowledge and skill of these experts right at your fingertips. Imagine you had to pay for their time! Well, you don't as here they offer you all the help and guidance you need to create your own successful website. This definitely gives the book a Wow Factor!

Whether you need to start a website from scratch or brush up and tweak an existing site - read the book from cover to cover. There is something in it for everyone - from a simple hobby site, an online presence right up to a full throttle internet business.

Technology doesn't stand still and you need to be on top of your game. We're an online nation and to be successful your website needs to do the business. This book will be your handy toolkit to show you how to create a successful website.

Best wishes for your website!

Claire Young

More About Claire

Claire Young, 31, is the straight talking, no-nonsense sales woman who infuriated and then won over 11 million viewers to reach the final in series 4 of BBC1's The Apprentice (2008).

Since then she has worked non-stop setting up numerous business ventures and is passionate about entrepreneurship and enterprise. Claire works regularly 'hands on' with young people delivering enterprise days in schools. She has also set up a social enterprise called www.girlsoutloud.org.uk, which works with 13-18 year girls helping to raise their aspirations.

One of her ventures is School Speakers, www.schoolspeakers.co.uk, launched 2010, which provides external speakers and workshops for schools.

She has become a regular presenter for GMTV; discusses business, employment and redundancy issues on Sky News and ITN; has become an established public speaker; and is now writing her own book! Claire writes a weekly newspaper column and contributes to a number of magazines.

After she graduated from Bristol University Claire accelerated up the career ladder. Before entering The Apprentice she worked in marketing for beauty giants L'Oreal, Colgate Palmolive and global health and beauty group, AS Watson.

Claire is passionate about working with young people, helping them to take off the blinkers and think big! Now a successful entrepreneur herself, she has a non-business background and hopes her story will motivate others; with hard work, drive and determination anything is possible.

She works with a number of organisations such as Aim Higher, Enterprise Village, Young Chamber of Commerce, National Apprenticeships, UK Youth, National Enterprise Academy, The Prince's Trust and Flying Start. On a personal note, Claire has physically transformed from her Apprentice days shedding 3.8 stone through diet and exercise.

Read about Claire at www.claireyoung.co.uk

Who Should Read This Book

Everyone

The world is moving so fast and getting smaller as the internet weaves an invisible social and business web around us. So this book is for everyone who wants to get online for personal and business reasons.

Do you want to start an online business and earn an extra income? Does your organisation or association need a web presence?

Or do you have a large, extended family scattered all over the world and want to start a project to keep everyone up to date with one website? Some topics specific to business may not interest you, but the info about how to do it yourself at hardly any cost will most certainly come in handy.

The book is also ideal for students (young and old) who want to slowly build up a profile or portfolio of their work. When I was freelancing, free blogs and easy do it yourself sites weren't around so now there's no excuse for anyone not to have an online presence.

Here's a quick list of who should read this book and why.

Artists and Creative People

Talented artists should be selling their work online. My sister's hubby is extremely talented and instead of waiting around for galleries to notice his work she set up a site to sell his work to the world at large. It's a great way to show off a portfolio without dragging a bunch of heavy canvases around town. Give your local gallery the link and ask them to choose which pieces they want to exhibit, if not all of them. Email regional and national galleries as well. And make sure you optimise your speciality website with keywords, such as traditional oils or contemporary watercolours.

Associations

There are countless associations that would benefit from getting online. A site with a few pages, either done with easy to use boxed software or a free blog site is the ideal tool to direct enquiries. Also, just being 'out there' gives people the ability to find your association when someone searches.

1

Actors and Sports Personalities

All up and coming athletes, swimmers, runners and all sports people with an ambition to see their name in lights at future Olympics should get themselves online. A website is the ideal platform for showing off your skills as a talented sports person.

Potential sponsors will be far more impressed if you can prove your value to them. If you start building a following through your site, they are also more likely to sponsor you. Check out the topic of sponsorship where we discuss generating revenue.

Similarly, actors who want to attract casting agents and film producers should have an online profile. This also goes for Amateur Dramatic Students who want to 'break' into the industry.

Authors and Writers

This is my personal favourite. Authors, writers and self published authors could do with a little peek into these pages to learn how to get visibility if they are not yet published. And if they are, they should be building a following where their readers are able to have some kind of personal contact with them.

Before I found a publisher for this book, I didn't have money for a grand site so I created a simple Wordpress blog with 'tabs' as my 'pages' to show off my writing material to potential publishers (paulawynne.wordpress.com). This can be converted into a full website when the need arises. I encourage all writers to give it a go.

Whether you are an established author promoting your books to a wider audience or a new writer peddling manuscripts to publishers and agents, having your own site will take your profile to the next level.

Emerging and new writers need to create a readership, which will help them get published. It's a superb way of introducing agents and publishers to you and your material, and if you can create a 'platform' of followers, readers and interest groups, you will be more valuable to a publisher one day.

This is my story. I established a business 'platform', which leveraged my proposal to publishers and led to me being commissioned to write this book. I aim to do the same for my novels.

Book Clubs

A simple little idea, such as a book club or reading group's website invites people to share a passion for similar interests. Post quick notices about past meetings or hook newcomers with enticing future reads. If you have a hankering for setting up *any* club, not just a book club, in your area, read on.

Churches

Even God is online. The obvious group to welcome new people into the fold will be a local church. All sorts of information can be posted freely through a blog or easy to use site. Some people may have the odd occasion to find a local church service to give thanks, such as Christmas. In times of grief, people are naturally drawn to God so churches can reach out to their local community by sharing details of their services and events online.

New and Established Business

Can I be so bold to say that it is a sin for any business, new or old, not to be online? I may be stretching my neck out here, but I look back at myself and crack a ruler over my own knuckles for all the time and business I lost by not getting online quicker. If only I had known how easy it was and that I could get it done free! I wish I'd had a book like this that showed me how to get online with quick, easy and, often free, advice.

This book is the perfect solution for you if you're thinking of setting up an online business or making the transition to get your current business online and growing it to 'the next level'.

Everyone has skills that could add a little extra income to the household. Whether it's a new full time business to replace your day job or a simple, small sideline business, you should read on.

Teach yourself how to create a successful website. Grab a coffee, put your feet up and snuggle down with this book and ample paper for scribbling notes. Or, you may prefer to have your laptop or PC handy to get more specific details into a Word or Excel document.

Career Hunters

Use the web to enhance your career. HR experts believe that a strong online image can help job hunters to land their dream job. A web presence should be carefully managed to create an online reputation that employers will see.

Community Groups

There is a wide diversity of cultural groups and communities that have been founded through an online presence. These communities work to welcome locals, share ethnic or cultural characteristics and discuss subjects affecting the people or community as a whole.

Some local communities may want to get online and maintain a 'localised' presence. Others may want to open their arms and build a larger following. Either way, common interests can also be discussed online in a virtual community where geography has no bounds.

eBay-ers

If you currently run an eBay site then it is worth having your own site, not only to show your products, but to instil trust in your buyers.

Many eBay-ers now realise the value in having a site connected to their eBay account so they can get the benefit of both worlds. Many thousands of users run an eBay business as their primary source of income, while cottage industries earn a secondary income from eBay. If this is you, why not take your earnings to the next level and create a site for your products? Keep your eBay account and use it to drive traffic to your new site.

Film Makers

Student and amateur film makers or indeed any film makers will get noticed and build credibility by setting up a web presence. Add all your film projects to your website and, with targeted optimisation, social interaction and publicity, your films will start to gain an audience of followers.

Graduates and Students

All graduates and students should consider setting up an online presence now, while you are studying, especially if you know which career path you will take.

> **FOR EXAMPLE:** as a budding web designer you can set up a site to contain images and a portfolio of the first sites you built. Not only will this be useful as a reminder of how far you have come, but blogging and building an optimised profile could help you to earn an income while studying. Plus, if you want to set up your own business one day, you will already have an established online presence.

Are you a fashion design student? How about showcasing a portfolio of your designs? They may not be well-known, but could earn a small income while at University and this could possibly become the foundation for a future fashion design business.

A word of warning, though; all students should be careful not to show drunken images of University life on your Facebook page. Many students upload all sorts of things without thinking or realising that future employers or potential clients may see their escapades as well!

Hobby-ists

Keen hobby-ists are gearing up for the net. More and more people who make their own crafts are sharing their passion with browsers who find their websites. If you have a hobby that is worth showing off, why not consider creating a website for it and see where your hobby could take you?

You may have no intention of making money from it, but just think of all the other people who enjoy the same or similar hobby and how you could all help each other, trade secrets, swap tips and converse.

Home Industry

If you bake cakes for your local area, maybe selling them in shops and pubs, have you considered setting up a website to show off what you do?

Craft specialists would also gain by having an online presence to act as a 'shop window' for selling hand made products. There are so many thousands of home industries, from cake making to specialist toy makers. They can all get online and work towards increasing visibility in a region.

Internet Entrepreneurs

A dead-end job, no money, redundancies, failed dreams, a failed marriage, seeing family suffer, dropping out of college and all manner of things can 'grow' an entrepreneur and turn them into a success. Don't wait for something to change your life. Get up and change it now!

"You are not born an entrepreneur, you grow into one."
Unknown

Practitioners

All practitioners and people offering health and beauty services should be online, especially those who feature a mobile service.

When I was having physiotherapy after a shoulder operation, I chatted away telling my therapist all about my site, what I was doing, how I was doing it and generally boring her, I thought, with all the daily routines. However, she was totally inspired by my chit chat and promptly went out and found someone to help her build a small site for her own business. This type of site may only be a few pages and could easily be done through a blog's free templates, which allow you to show page tabs so it looks like a 'proper' website. Practitioners can establish a local following by optimising their geographical regions.

Professionals and Freelancers

All professionals, freelancers, experts and consultants should be building an online profile, not just with Social Media, but with your own website. It is a great way to capitalise on your expertise and generate new revenue streams for your freelance business. The same goes for anyone who wants to be head-hunted and climb the corporate ladder. Don't only show off a LinkedIn profile. With your own free website you can control the areas of your CV you want to feature with your own landing page. Get found by the best employers and outsourcers - or go one better and send your ideal boss an email with a link to your website. You will WOW their socks off!

Party Plan Agents

There is a hive of micro home based businesses who work in the direct selling arena. If you're an agent or distributor running your own home business then show off your wares to local and regional customers and even run an online party booking service.

Retailers

The web is an obvious place for a retailer to 'open' an all day 'shop window', so it is surprising to find out how many are still not online.

Even if you can't afford a fancy online shop to accommodate all your products, you should at least have a small site and provide contact details to encourage people to buy your items and re-order. It's better to have a small profile than none at all.

If you are starting a retail outlet online, you'll need a secure e-commerce shopping cart, product catalogue, web store admin tools and the all essential secure transaction protection. See the section about how to set up an online shop later. There's some exciting stuff in there!

Trades People

People who specialise in a trade, such as Plumbers, Electricians and Carpet Fitters must get themselves online pretty damn quick. Just because a 'man-in-white-van' claims his place of work is out in the field, that's no reason why he can't shout about his service via a website. Most people 'Google' trade services and, with all the free and easy ways to get online, there's no better time.

A to Z

No matter who you are or what your reasons are, if you need some assistance to get online, this book is for you. If you have no idea where to turn on a PC or you are 'old school' and a computer terrifies you then why not get a son, daughter, or even a grandchild involved? Show them this book, and ask them to help you get online. Maybe gift wrap it for them with a note inside asking for help. And they can get themselves online too!

Finally

Throughout the book I may refer to the words 'your business' or 'your company', however this includes agencies, churches, associations, individuals, communities, practitioners and graduates.

If you class your website as a business and look at it that way, it will give you more focus to ensure its success. So when I say 'your business', this encompasses everyone else that I have mentioned here, even if you have more of a project than an actual business. Whatever you do, your venture will be referred to as your online business.

Introductions

Introducing The Book

This is not a developer's website guide nor does it teach HTML (hypertext markup language - the code used to write web pages). Instead, it provides an easy-to-follow roadmap for anyone setting up a website, an online shop, business or trade.

Create A Successful Website will guide you through the mine-field of website building, instant sites, online jargon and confusing technology. And it will teach you how to find the right avenue for your brilliant website concept!

This book will not show you how to make millions overnight or give you insider secrets to get rich schemes. None of that malarkey here! Instead, the book guides you step-by-step from research and planning your website right through to revenue options.

CHART YOUR SUCCESS

The idea behind this book is to provide a down-to-earth way to answer the questions and concerns that new business 'Start Ups' face, and in particular we will focus on the DIY angle to save costs by doing lots of essential tasks in-house. More importantly, it will give your business an online blueprint from day one or even before you start.

What do I mean by online blueprint? Simple, an outline of your online presence, and all you have to do to achieve one. It will become your online strategy, enhance your business plan and act as the backbone to your online business or website concept. Your blueprint will also be a source of encouragement and inspiration to you as a fledging entrepreneur. Every step you take brings you closer to your dreams and ambitions, so looking back at what you've accomplished will spur you on to create more successes.

CHECKLISTS AND NOTES

A quick scan or flick through the pages will show you daily checklists for each topic. They will guide you and ensure you have completed all your tasks. There is even a handy little tick box beside each item so you can cross them off your list.

TIP WATCH

As well as quotes and examples, watch out for the following symbols that point to expert advice, hot tips and jargon busters.

 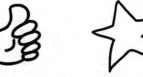

JARGON BUSTER   **TOP TIP**   **EXPERT ADVICE**

HOW TO USE THE DIY METHOD

The aim of this book is to fuel your passion and enthusiasm for your online presence, inspire you to become an authority and expert in your chosen sector and give you all the tools you need to create a successful website.

At the end of this book you will have a complete strategy for your website. Most of the hard work will be done and you will only need to implement the plan with finishing touches. After finishing the book you should have a workable plan which will excite you to continue on this journey you have set for yourself.

The book is broken down into bite size pieces with days instead of chapters. Each day gives you various topics and tasks with easy to follow steps and visuals - the quickest way to understand without having to dissect all the geeky jargon.

WORK IT BABY, WORK IT

I can hear you already thinking: "How on earth am I going to stick to this daily schedule?"

Don't worry, you don't have to. It is only there to guide you. You may want to do a few days in one go or you may be compelled to race ahead and get it all done at once. Find what works best for you and stick to that formula. It goes without saying that you will also need bucket loads of energy, enthusiasm and motivation as well as tons of passion and determination!

Introducing Me

As websites show the important 'About Us' page, I wanted to give you a little intro to me and the experiences that have led me to writing this book.

However, before I do that I wanted to firstly say THANK YOU for choosing this book.

POTHOLE JOURNEY

At the end of this book, you will be fully equipped to avoid the potholes that many new start ups have stumbled upon along their way to creating a successful website .

Use this book as a guide to give you a good foundation in which to direct your new online business.

DIY ACTIVIST

For 'privacy and permissions' reasons, I have used my own sites in examples and visuals. In some instances I have been able to use screenshots from our expert's sites. Use these illustrations to think laterally and keep your eyes peeled for similar cases when browsing the web.

I also wanted to assure you that this book is written by a user, a 'Do It Yourself' (DIY) Activist, or you could say a previous-beginner.

I love every minute of learning and I'm pleased to say that I am *still* learning. I want to get the message across that everyone - men and women, younger and older generations - should get online. So, with this book, I want to motivate and inspire others to reach out and get themselves online successfully!

IN A NUTSHELL

The 'about me' used when I talk to groups of people at seminars or conferences goes along these lines:

"After a career as a publicist and marketer, Paula Wynne is now an award-winning businesswoman, an online entrepreneur, woman's ambassador and speaker.

"She aims to help others to work flexibly, as she has needed to do, and Remote Employment is her and her partner's vision for bringing a better quality work life to working parents across the UK. Their 'Home Working World' aims to connect home workers and home businesses across the globe and unite them in a supportive community. Paula is also the organiser of the unique and popular Remote Worker Awards and is a SEEDA Women's Enterprise Ambassador."

BEHIND THE SCENES

In January 2008 I co-founded Remote Employment and have achieved success as an online entrepreneur.

Google's No 1

In just over a year, Remote Employment became Google's No 1 both in the UK and Worldwide for our key-words, namely 'Flexible Jobs' and 'Home Based Jobs', which beats 192 million searches daily! We are proud to have forged our way through some of the most competitive keywords in the world in such a short time.

AWARD WINNING

Our company has won two Business Awards. Our first award was the BT Small Business Week 'Responsible Business Day' Award. Our second came shortly after, where I was awarded Karen Darby as my mentor!

Imagine having a serial entrepreneur and one of the UK's most successful businesswomen as a mentor! Read more about Karen at her website www.karendarbydirect.com.

Remote Employment was also nominated as a Top 100 Company in the Barclays Trading Places Award. We are Runner Up in The Enterprise Challenge of the Enterprising Women Awards 2009 and Finalist in the Best Online Business in the Women on their Way Awards.

LEARN FROM OUR MISTAKES, NOT YOURS

Many internet entrepreneurs toss out their first website and waste valuable time and money before they have a workable online solution.

Ontrapment

Online beginners don't have to fall into that trap anymore. With this book you'll have the tools and guidance you need to create a successful online presence.

A point that strikes me constantly when I talk at events, seminars and conferences, is that so many people are in the same shoes I was in not so long ago. This book will clear the path so you don't make the mistakes that I, and many other online entrepreneurs, have made .

Outlaws

To make matters worse, there are no rules or governing bodies to stop outlaws and cowboys charging for websites that will not perform in the rankings and thus quash new entrepreneurial dreams. This book will provide you with the tools to spot a fake from a genuine expert.

Introducing Our Expert Panel

I have gathered together the 'crème-de-la-entrepreneurial-crème', who have generously agreed to share their business knowledge and online experience with you. Get to know them by checking out their biography and brief business summaries before you read their advice.

JO HAIGH, AUTHOR & HEAD OF CORPORATE FINANCE, MGR
BUSINESS: *fds* Group and MGR
WEBSITE: www.jo-haigh.com
TYPE OF SITE: Business Advisors

Jo Haigh is a Partner and Head of Corporate Finance for The ATF Group; a company based in London and Yorkshire, and a partner in the *fds* Group, a specialist training and development business.

Jo has a long list of Awards, Titles and Achievements, and she is a bestselling author. Jo's first book, *The Business Rules*, published 2005 has been such a success that a foreign rights deal has been confirmed with a publisher in China. Jo's second book, *An Entrepreneur's Guide*, and her third book, *Tales from the Glass Ceiling - A Survival Guide for Women in Business*, sold out of its first reprint after 5 days. It was also the best selling business book of the year 2008 selling over 500,000 copies.

Jo's Dos:

- ✓ Do make sure you have sufficient cash.
- ✓ Do take the best advice you can afford.
- ✓ Do know your market.

Jo's Don'ts:

- ✗ Don't go into Partnership or start a company without an approved Shareholder or Partnership Agreement in place.
- ✗ Don't assume because *you* love it, everyone else will.
- ✗ Don't be a pessimist or optimist – be a realist.

14

KAREN HANTON, CHIEF EXECUTIVE, TOPTABLE

BUSINESS: Toptable
WEBSITE: www.toptable.com
TYPE OF SITE: Restaurant booking service

From her initial training and career in HR, Karen has founded and developed a number of successful ventures over the past 15 years. Karen is widely known within the industry as a pioneer within new media, regularly lecturing on the subject and coaching young entrepreneurs. She has also received significant public recognition including the Financial Times/Moet Hennessy Extraordinary Achievers Award, named as one of today's top 30 entrepreneurs in New Business Magazine and named one of the top 100 most influential people in the first decade of the internet in an NOP/e-consultancy poll. As the biggest online restaurant booking service in Europe, the website lists around 5,000 restaurants in 14 countries and gets 2.3 million visits a month. Karen has now sold Toptable in a £35million deal with US restaurant reservation service OpenTable Inc.

Karen's Dos:

- ✓ Do your research no matter how crude.
- ✓ Track progress and set yourself some KPI's (Key Performer Indicators).
- ✓ Give yourself a set time to 'prove' your model.
- ✓ Your site has to be compelling and useful, and this has to be immediately obvious when the person visits your site.

Karen's Don'ts:

- ✗ Don't front load your business with big fixed costs.
- ✗ Don't blindly carry on when it is obvious it isn't working.
- ✗ Don't try to reinvent the wheel. Most things have some similarities – take the smart course and save yourself time.
- ✗ Don't compete against millions of other sites and things like social networks which swallow huge amounts of potential consumer browsing time.

POLLY GOWERS, FOUNDER, EVERYCLICK.COM
BUSINESS: Everyclick
WEBSITE: www.everyclick.com
TYPE OF SITE: Charity

Polly founded Everyclick.com, the website that enables consumers to give to any UK charity in the way that they want. Everyclick.com is a search engine that gives half of its revenue to charity. Its technology has been specifically created to provide a sustainable, no cost fundraising tool for all charities. It provides any internet user with a free and hassle-free way to raise money for the charity of their choice. Polly was voted WEBA Ethical Entrepreneur of the Year 2007 and a Blackberry Woman in Technology Award winner in 2008. Everyclick.com was voted website of the Year 2008 and was nominated as a Media Tech 100 company 2009.

Polly's Dos:

- ✓ Plan.
- ✓ Plan.
- ✓ Execute.

Polly's Don'ts:

- ✗ Don't 'not' have a plan.
- ✗ Don't waste your time trying to sell advertising.

MAX BENSON, MBE, CO-FOUNDER, EVERYWOMAN

BUSINESS: Everywoman
WEBSITE: www.everywoman.com
TYPE OF SITE: Women's Networking Community

Max Benson MBE is co-founder of everywoman, one of the leading global brands for women in business. Everywoman understands what resources and support services women in business need in order to realise their business ambitions. She is one of the UK's leading advocates for women in business and female entrepreneurs, Max has first-hand experience of the challenges small business owners encounter as they start and grow their ventures and has attracted the attention of corporate partners including IBM, NatWest and BT.

Max was appointed MBE in the 2009 New Year Honours, in recognition of her service to women's enterprise.

Max's Dos:

- ✓ Bring in technical expertise.
- ✓ Get it up. Don't wait to get your website perfect, it will always be a 'work in progress'.
- ✓ Complete your marketing mix; make sure all aspects are right.

Max's Don'ts:

- ✗ Don't fear technology, think of it as a tool to enable your vision not something to dread.
- ✗ Don't focus on every last small detail and try to get it correct, it's actually all about user experience not your personal bug bears. You'll never get it 100%.
- ✗ Don't worry about wrong turns and mistakes, the important thing is to just correct them and move on.

CARRIE LONGTON, CO-FOUNDER, MUMSNET

BUSINESS: Mumsnet.com
WEBSITE: www.mumsnet.com
TYPE OF SITE: Parenting Community

Mumsnet was set up in January 2000 by Justine Roberts, a sports journalist, and Carrie Longton, a TV producer. Inspired by their antenatal class group as the best source of information on everything from sleep problems to choosing first shoes, Justine and Carrie wanted to build a much larger circle of parents sharing their know-how on the net. Mumsnet Towers is staffed by mums working flexibly part time. Their philosophy is simple: To make parents' lives easier by pooling knowledge and experience.

Carrie's Dos:
- ✓ Make sure your site is easy to navigate and works.
- ✓ Be prepared to adapt and evolve with changing technology.
- ✓ Find a niche that needs filling and fill it.
- ✓ Make sure you understand SEO (Search Engine Optimisation) and use it.
- ✓ Encourage your users to help you market your site, make as much use as you can of positive feedback and the press.
- ✓ Make sure your idea is new, interesting, and useful and has a potential revenue stream.
- ✓ Ask advice from anyone who has been there before.
- ✓ Keep costs low to start with and expect to put in a lot of hours!

Carrie's Don'ts:
- ✗ Don't take on too many overheads before you know you can make a living.
- ✗ Don't give away too much equity early on.
- ✗ Don't lose control of your brand.
- ✗ Without having business expertise, don't be afraid to ask questions.
- ✗ Don't be afraid of employing good people who might know more than you!
- ✗ Don't skimp on childcare if you have a young family – you need all the help you can get.

DEBBIE BIRD, EDITOR, BABYWORLD

BUSINESS: Babyworld
WEBSITE: www.babyworld.co.uk
TYPE OF SITE: Baby Community

Debbie is the Editor of babyworld.co.uk, the UK's leading online Parenting Magazine, and knows how essential advice sites are to new parents. She is responsible for the creation of all editorial content for the site, which currently has around 20,000 pages. She aims to develop and improve the site over the next year, updating the advice and positively moving the site into the next decade. Debbie was awarded "Highly Commended" in the Home Worker Award Category in the Remote Home Workers Award 2009.

Debbie's Dos:

- ✓ Keep true to your core business. It is easy to think you can cover everything, yet you can risk diluting the main purpose of your site if you spread yourself too thinly.
- ✓ Keep your site up to date, but not dated. Be careful to post information that will not date you. Unless you are a news site where topics change and move all the time, be careful not to age yourself by putting dates and names on everything.
- ✓ Plan your website.
- ✓ Research your subject.
- ✓ Embrace the knowledge of those who have done it before.

Debbie Don'ts:

- ✗ Don't rush your website.
- ✗ Don't ignore search engine's requirements.
- ✗ Don't think search engines are the enemy, work with them.

JON BUXTON, OPERATIONS DIRECTOR, BABYWORLD

BUSINESS: Babyworld
WEBSITE: www.babyworld.co.uk
TYPE OF SITE: Baby Community

Jon joined Babyworld in July 1999, prior to which he was the Product Manager for the IT security cluster at Elsevier Advanced Technology. He has also held positions in Finance, Purchasing, Retailing, Customer Services and IT.

Jon has turned his hand to network administration, marketing, e-commerce, graphic design, customer service and operations - sometimes all on the same day.

Jon's Dos:

- ✓ There are no shortcuts. Get the basics right. There are no prizes for having the flashiest website around, particularly if it doesn't generate any traffic or revenue.
- ✓ Make sure your site is easy to read, easy on the eye, and is not full of typing errors as it reflects badly on you as a company (makes people think that you don't really care).
- ✓ Think about your audience. They are looking for a solution whether it is a product or some information or advice. Make sure your website provides them with that solution.
- ✓ Do plenty of research on the web. Work out which sites appeal to you and why. Talk to some potential customers and find out what they are looking for.

Jon's Don'ts:

- ✗ Don't spend thousands of pounds on marketing campaigns to drive traffic before making sure your website is constructed in a "Google friendly" way.
- ✗ Don't build your site and then think about SEO. Think about Search Engine Optimisation before you start designing and writing your website. Good SEO is much harder to achieve if you only think about it after you have built your site.

CLARE MEDDEN, MEDDEN DESIGN

BUSINESS: Medden Website Design
WEBSITE: www.medden.co.uk
TYPE OF SITE: Website Developer

Clare Medden worked for over 10 years in advertising. After a short break to have two children, Clare began her career in the world of website design. Four years on, and Medden Website Design is flourishing. The company prides itself on offering a friendly and reliable service and strives to create websites that are both individual, expandable and future proof.

Clare's Dos:

- ✓ Research, Research, Research – when choosing any professionals to help you, you cannot do enough research. You must take the time to find the right services for you.
- ✓ Find a niche – find something that others are not doing or are not doing well and do it better.
- ✓ Enjoy the feeling of that first sale and use that feeling to put more back into your business.
- ✓ Keep true to your core business.
- ✓ Specialise. Don't try to be all things to all people.
- ✓ Make contact with a website developer, even if it's just for advice.
- ✓ Above all have fun – it's not good going into an online business or getting a business online if you aren't going to enjoy it. Yes, you may cry at some of your mistakes, but pick yourself up and you will laugh at them one day.

Clare's Don'ts:

- ✗ Don't follow the herd. Think for yourself and don't be frightened to try something new.
- ✗ Make sure your domain is registered in your name. Clare says: "I can't tell you how many redesigns I have done and found out that people had no contract with their existing developer and that we have a problem getting the domain signed over to them."
- ✗ Don't rest on your laurels and think that you know it all. The internet is an ever-changing industry and anyone who thinks they know it all and does not need to keep up to date will soon be seen as extinct as the dinosaurs.

Day 1: Planning & Research

Essential Prep

Today is all about planning, researching and brainstorming. We will talk about setting short and long term goals and objectives for your site to steer you in the right direction. We'll also discuss options for managing your online business and watching for competitors.

IINSPIRE JUICY THOUGHT PATTERNS
- ✓ Print off your plan and take it with you
- ✓ Add more details when on the train or bus
- ✓ Scan the notes, then drift into creative mode
- ✓ Having your plan with you, will give you an organised way to edit and pump up your website.

You will learn how to analyse your strengths and weaknesses as well as any potential threats and most importantly, the opportunities that raise their heads.

As you plan your shiny new website, you will understand the need to explore every avenue of your online business so that you are fully prepared. The work you do now will be reinforced along the way.

Polly Gowers from Everyclick believes that running a business is like playing a game of snakes and ladders. She says: "It can be the roll of the dice that takes you to the top snake or ladder. However, I have learned that the better the team you gather around you, the easier you find the ladders."

Naming Your Site

By now you'll have an idea for your website; it could have been stewing away in your brain for many years or it may have only popped in for a visit recently and something made you pounce on it.

Before we go into planning your site, one of the first things to consider is the name. Many entrepreneurs have realised the viral effect naming can have on a business. When you go through the process of brainstorming a name, you will come up with all sorts of concoctions.

Your Name Could:

✓ Be a synopsis of your business concept
✓ Use a key message or catch phrase
✓ Include keywords
✓ Be a type of business

✗ Don't copy competitors

I suggest you come back to your name when you have finished all the chapters in this book.

 KAREN HANTON FROM TOPTABLE ADVISES...

✓ Do some simple research to make sure you have a market for your product, however simple.

✓ You can come up with a sample consumer group from friends, relatives and neighbours that will cost a lot less than a McKinsey report and will probably give you just as accurate a result.

Domain Names

Firstly, there are a multitude of sites from which you can buy a domain name. Many of them will offer hosting as well.

If you aim to set up an instant site (more on this soon), use their domain and hosting service all in one if you can, just to make life easier. They may also provide pop boxes for a personalised email – which I definitely recommend. Have you seen a professional site with an email address along the lines of: aname123@hotmail.com or anotherexample@btconnect.com? Would you recognise that business as trustworthy and solid or as a 'one person band'? Point taken. So when you're buying your domain, get yourself an email that reflects and brands your website's domain.

The most important thing about domain names is: firstly you MUST own it and secondly, find a name that you can use for viral and optimisation purposes as well. Before you rush off and buy up a hoard of names, as I have done in the past, and then sit with useless domains, let's consider some factors that go into choosing a domain.

- A POP Box is a nifty way to ensure that your email matches your company name. Because you are not online 24/7 your emails are caught and stored in a 'box' on your ISP's server until you do come online.
- Your mail program (Outlook Express, Netscape, Eudora, Pegasus, etc.) logs into your POP3 mail box via your local access provider to read your mail. Each POP account requires a unique username and password to access the mail.

Successful Domain Names

You may want to buy a name for an existing business, thus you need to get that exact name, or something similar if it is already taken.

If you are choosing a name to reflect a brand then make sure it is short, clear and easy to spell. I would suggest you buy both the .com and the .co.uk and any others that protects your brand in future.

If you cannot get the exact name you want you may need to have a fiddle with – (dashes). If your best choice is taken for a .co.uk or .com, search with Geek Tools for a better choice to get a primary domain. See the notes on Geek Tools in the next section.

Better still – choose a descriptive, keyword-rich domain name. Google favours these domains in its rankings for searches that are based on those exact words. If it isn't possible to get the perfect keyword-rich domain name you desire, you can use keywords in the URL. We did that before we were able to transfer our site to a better performing SEO architecture.

> **FOR EXAMPLE:** we used the term work from home after the domain, which went something like:
> www.remoteemployment.com/work-from-home/contact us

International V Country Domains

A .com gives your site international appeal, whereas a .co.uk shows that you are a UK based company. .co.za will tell your visitors that your services and products are mainly for the South African market. The same goes for any other country fixture.

There is nothing stopping you choosing any country fixture, it is completely your decision based on your long term goals and aspirations for your new site.

Here are some of the domain names that you will come across when researching names. Along with .com and .net, .org is one of the original global domain names.

GENERIC

- **.COM:** the most famous and popular global domain name. It was originally created for commercial websites, but has developed into the preferred first choice for any type of website
- **.GOV.UK:** mainly for the UK government sector
- **.AC.UK:** used for educational purposes like universities, colleges and schools
- **.ORG:** for non profit organisations and charities
- **.BIZ:** mostly for business use
- **.INFO:** originally created for global information websites
- **.NET:** was originally created for use by technical websites. It is often used when a .com is unavailable, or to protect brands that already have the .com.

COUNTRY DOMAINS

- **.CO.UK:** for UK sites, they often register both .com and .co.uk
- **.EU:** is used within the European Union
- **.IM:** is for the Isle of Man!
- **.BE:** is the extension for Belgium
- **.DE:** is the country code for Germany
- **.MX:** is the country code for Mexico
- **.CO.AU:** is the country code for Australia
- **.CO.NZ:** is the country code for New Zealand
- **.PL:** is the country code for Poland
- **.IN:** is the country code for India
- **.CO.ZA:** is the country code for South Africa

And the list goes on...

MOBI

Mobi is one of the newest top level domain names. It is aimed specifically at companies, organisations and individuals wanting to create websites and services for mobile devices.

An individual, organisation or company must ensure that any site using a .mobi domain name:

- Is built using compliant mobile code
- Responds to requests from mobile devices at its primary URL
- Does not use frames

.ME.UK

This code was created with individuals in mind, .me.uk is great for those who want to create a more personal domain name, but please note that .me.uk domains can only be registered by individuals.

> **FOR EXAMPLE:** students who aim to get a top job can set up a .me site and list all of their achievements.

.EU

The .eu domain name is one of the most popular domains for companies, organisations and individuals within the European Union. An individual, organisation or company must comply with the following:

- Have its registered office, central administration or principal place of business within the Community
- Be an organisation established within the Community without prejudice to the application of national law
- Be a natural person resident within the Community
- Exclude domains on the blocked or reserved list

Geek Tools

Another handy thing to know is how to find available domains and, at the same time, keep your search for them hidden to prevent your cool domain from being snatched up before you get the chance to buy it.

Use www.geektools.com, click in the far right hand corner on the link called 'Whois' to see if certain words are already taken as domain names.

This screenshot shows that you can enter some ideas for names and then see if someone else has that domain name already. The full name including the domain tail was too long for me to show you, but you should also add the fixture such as .com

or .co.uk onto the name to provide a full search. The end results show you the person who owns that name; otherwise it comes up with 0 results if the name is still available.

Hosting

It seems natural to talk about hosting right after domains, as you would naturally buy a domain and hosting together or you would find a company to host your domain. However, you may be able to get hosting included in a free website package and a pay monthly website. And, of course, your developer can arrange this for you too.

Once you have established what kind of site you are going to have you can tackle hosting. Before signing up to the first provider that comes along, add these questions to your research list as you will need to find either the best deal or the best support package.

HOSTING QUESTIONS

❑ How much web space will you need to store even the most basic website? Remote Employment has thousands of pages and a site of this size could be costly.

❑ Remember your future plans and how successful your site could become. What will you need in the coming months and years?

❑ Will your site require video, podcasts and other multimedia applications? If so, check that the hosting provider can supply this.

❑ Will you need support? If something goes wrong does it matter to you whether your provider is UK or overseas based? Even though our first developer was only a few miles down the road, our site toppled over once and we couldn't get hold of him to sort it out on a Sunday. These things happen!

❑ Will you need email pop boxes?

❑ Will you need regular back up?

❑ Will members be uploading content? Are there uploading restrictions?

Hosting fees can be high, and they are normally paid for in advance, so do shop around. I suggest you read the Free Websites, Hosted Websites and Bespoke Website chapters before you decide on hosting as the information in these chapters may help to determine which option you should go for and, therefore, if you need separate hosting or not.

Score Goals

If you haven't already done so, you will need to set goals and objectives. This way you can establish the exact aim of the business. You may have grand plans to sell this brilliant idea of yours for a cash bomb with an exit strategy after a number of years. You might want to manage a small and cosy family business over a long period. Maybe you need to run your online business while working a day job or alongside another business.

Whatever it is you want to do, you need to aspire to something in order to achieve it. Recognition of your aspirations and actually visualising it, will lead to achievement and result in success.

My mentor, Karen Darby, inspires people when she tells them that she started visualising her ideal home. Then, when she sold her business, SimplySwitch, to the Daily Mail for £22m she found the house of her dreams and was pleasantly surprised to find it matched her imagined home.

You too can picture where you want to go and what you want to do with your website. In tough times recall this image and renew your determination to make it work. The best way to get somewhere is to want it badly enough!

Hey BIG Thinker

While considering your aspirations for your new online business we are cooking up together, be positive and always aim high.

You will achieve far more in life if you reach for the sky. Don't be afraid to fail. More importantly, don't fail to start. If you aim half way up the ladder, you may reach just below the half way mark, yet if you aim above 75%, you could achieve more than 50 or 60%. So dream big dreams and think big thoughts.

It took time for Remote Employment to become Google's No 1 for 'Flexible Jobs', but we have always aimed to be the biggest and best site for flexible and home based working. We are now in the running to become the global leader for remote and home based jobs!

*"Don't expect to make money straight away.
Do your research and make sure there's a
market for your business."*
Carrie Longton, Mumsnet

As we go along you will be reminded of your goals and aspirations. When we chat about branding I will give you some ideas about thinking differently in order to become a BIG player. So when you plan your goals think BIG and believe you can achieve whatever you set out to do. In saying that, don't delude yourself in believing you can become an instant overnight millionaire. If that happens, brilliant, but it's better to prepare for a longer journey and some hard work!

At the end of today's chapter, make a start on your goals. I would strongly suggest you keep scribbling away at them as you go along because each day covers important details, hints and tips that will bring you back to your goal setting.

Keep this book in your bag or briefcase or take a notebook everywhere you go and as inspiration floats by, grab it and write down your thoughts.

An example of a goal could be to finish this book within a certain time frame, to complete your research within 7 days, to hold meetings with prospective developers by the end of the month or to possibly set up weekly project meetings with the key members of your online team.

Once you have a BIG dream for your business, set goals and objectives to achieve that vision. Have these goals and targets visible, possibly on a notice board above your desk, in a spreadsheet, in your calendar or even on a fridge magnet. Just keep them handy so you can monitor and measure progress on a regular basis.

Business Plans

If you are aiming to start a business that will have 'legs' and stick around for many years, you should also write out a full business plan. There are many organisations to help you as well as online resources to tap into. Some banks also offer this service to new business start ups. Although I would like to go into detail about what to feature in a successful business plan, I simply don't have the space here, as I need to give you more elements on how to set up a thriving website.

USP

A Unique Selling Proposition (USP) is described in Philip Kotler's book *Principles of Marketing*, as the unique product benefit that a firm aggressively promotes in a consistent manner to its target audience. The benefit usually reflects functional superiority: best quality, best services, lowest price and most advanced technology.

Check Wikipedia's USP Examples:

- Head & Shoulders: "You get rid of dandruff"
- Olay: "You get younger-looking skin"
- Domino's Pizza: "You get fresh, hot pizza delivered to your door in 30 minutes or less -- or it's free."

- FedEx: "When your package absolutely, positively has to get there overnight"
- More: http://en.wikipedia.org/wiki/Unique_selling_proposition

Now Get SMART

You may have heard people sprouting about SMART goals. Although the acronym has a number of slightly different variations, in short, it means your goals are Specific, Measurable, Attainable, Realistic and Time Limited.

SPECIFIC

Don't just say you want to set up your online business this year. Say that you want to set it up within the next three months. Or, better still, set a launch date. A general goal would suggest: "Set up my online business."

A specific goal would state: "Launch my online business by 29 January." Also try and stretch yourself by using this type of declaration to inspire you or boot you into action.

MEASURABLE

Measure your progress with meaningful goals and milestones. This way you will stay on target and experience the excitement of achievement, which will motivate and urge you to reach your goal.

ATTAINABLE

To attain, reach or accomplish your goal, plan your steps and create a time frame. When I set goals for this book to be published, I created a spreadsheet in Excel and as I targeted publishers, I literally ticked them off the list. I am sure you can guess that I am a 'list person'!

RELEVANT AND REALISTIC

Your goal will be realistic if you truly believe that it can be done and you know what it will take to accomplish it. When my partner and I decided to be Google's No 1 for flexible jobs, we had no idea what it would take and I set myself a steep learning curve (hey ho, what fun we've had).

Be reasonable with yourself and, above all, be rewarding. Give yourself little treats when you reach different milestones and share it with your family. It will gain their support for your idea.

FOR EXAMPLE: whenever we reach even a small step in the right direction, we buy ourselves a mega coffee, a lunch or even a dinner. You may even set aside outings with friends and family.

How good would your son feel if you told him that you were going to play footie with him after school on Friday? Whatever the treat, the feel-good factor makes you work harder.

TIMELY

By setting a track-able time frame with an exact date, you have set your mind into gear. Without you being aware, it will be quietly working away at reaching the goal date. Setting a time also cunningly gives you a sense of urgency to ensure you keep making progress.

Define Your Strengths and Weaknesses

A SWOT Analysis is a way to plan and assess the Strengths, Weaknesses, Opportunities, and Threats involved in starting and running your website. Once you know the objectives for your website, you can consider positive and negative aspects of your plan.

Identifying your SWOTs is crucial because you can take steps during your planning to overcome a weakness or lessen a threat. It will also establish your strengths and opportunities and spark creative ideas for marketing.

It is particularly helpful to bring to light any future development and possible growth plans.

> **FOR EXAMPLE:** after we launched Remote Employment, we went back to our SWOT and explored ways to increase our strengths and diminish any weaknesses or threats. So we launched an Awards site honouring individuals and companies who champion remote and home working.

Polly Gowers from Everyclick advises that you be clear about what your objectives are and what it is you need your customer to do. Everyclick is all about enabling the user to support their favourite charity so they make sure their content is highly personalised to support their favourite cause. See this in action below where Everyclick has personalised an RSPB page.

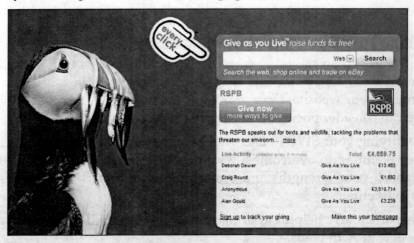

SWOT = AKA Sweat Analysis

Ideally, a SWOT analysis starts with defining a desired end objective, it's a sweaty old task, but someone's gotta do it.

STRENGTHS

List out qualities of your online business or website that will help achieve your business objectives. Remember to include resources, such as yourself or business partners. Your and their strengths are important to your venture.

> **FOR EXAMPLE:** my background is PR and this 'strength' played an important role in reaching a wider audience and overcame one of our weaknesses, a limited marketing budget. So use a strength to combat a weakness.

WEAKNESSES

This could be the actions or activities of you, your business partners and your company that may hinder achievement.

OPPORTUNITIES

This is fun: list out positive external or internal factors that will assist in achieving your plan.

> **FOR EXAMPLE:** in our SWOT, advances in technology were regarded as a big opportunity for more people working from home. Then, when the recession hit, despite it being a negative it turned to a positive opportunity as many people who were faced with redundancy now wanted alternative ways of working.

THREATS

Negative outer or inner factors that could potentially do damage to your online business.

> **FOR EXAMPLE:** when we launched The Remote Worker Awards and were looking for headline sponsors, these were brief and basic SWOTs:
>
> - **STRENGTHS:** unique, new, sexiness of the remote working concept, huge PR opportunity.
> - **WEAKNESS:** no track record, therefore harder to crack big sponsors.
> - **OPPORTUNITIES:** Award Categories could be branded with a company's name, along with a high profile judging panel.
> - **THREATS:** some sponsors may have the view that because it was the inaugural Awards, that the idea could potentially fail.

We took our Opportunities and Strengths to the extreme and managed to get more than £891k in positive PR media coverage. The campaign doubled our site traffic! The moral of the SWOT story – take your S and O and go hell for leather to reduce the W and T.

It is a good idea to look at the 'order of magnitude'. If the S and Os are a lot bigger than the W and Ts, put most of your effort into them or vice versa. And don't underestimate the T of your competition – know their S and Ws.

Your SWOT analysis will help you use lateral thinking to get the most creative ideas into your plans. As you get further embedded into this book and more light bulbs go off in your head, keep coming back to this section and add to your SWOT. It is a constantly revolving and evolving piece of work.

Revolve and Evolve

Babyworld was set up to provide medical and expert advice and has developed over the past 11 years. It now aims to deliver information and advice for parents so they can make informed choices about all areas of being parents with totally unbiased information on a wide area of topics.

> *"Everywoman's evolution has been driven by the needs of our community."*
> Max Benson, MBE everywoman

Similarly, the 'everywoman' website has changed constantly over the past ten years. It has had many incarnations, but their mission has remained the same; they always support women in business.

Competitive Analysis

While you want to beat the competitive guys over the road, you don't want to copy them, so find out what they do best and worst. Ensure that there is no fuzzy confusion with their site and yours by avoiding the same colours, fonts and designs. Of course, it goes without saying, never use their key message. Yours must be distinctly different and unique to your business. Don't try and wear too many hats - in other words, focus on a niche or speciality. This will give you the competitive edge.

SPY SPOTTING

When you spy on your competitors, establish what makes you different from them and why your visitors should buy from you. Also figure out what model they use and how you could follow the best of something similar without being a copy cat. Best of all – be original and creative, and only use them to gauge your SWOT. In doing so, you will rise above them.

BRAINSTORMING

In order to get yourself prepared for your website, research your market's industry sector and brainstorm different inventive ways to show off your products. The act of brainstorming doesn't always have to be at a wipe board, in front of a PC or surrounded by your notes. Once you start the process of brainstorming your unconscious mind and creative thought processes will be working intensely to decipher the issues you need solving.

For a long time I have written novels and whenever the idea for a new book pops into my head, my brain chomps on the idea and it develops over time. Then, when I get down to the planning process, I am chuffed to see how much has been brewing upstairs. Keep your bubbling pot going and carry on making notes. As you go through this book, bursts of meaty detail will come to light.

iMindMap

A cool tool to brainstorm is mind mapping. Buzan's iMindMap is an organic thinking experience. This brainy piece of software hosts a range of features designed to make you more productive and creative in the way you think.

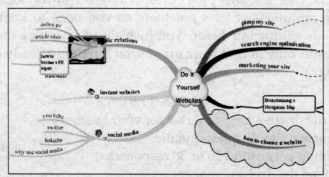

It's like a giant Octopus with colourful tentacles, images and icons that allow you to add notes and links to a range of files.

When brainstorming chapters for this book, I tried iMindMap Ultimate, which helps you to generate new ideas quickly and effectively and most importantly, to store them in an organised way. It helps to plan and record spontaneous bursts of inspiration, as well as to explore promotions for your future website.

This piece of software is just what the doctor ordered for your navigation map, which we cover in our next chapter. The computer age is so exciting and innovative. With this kind of cutting-edge technology writers, promoters, marketers and planners - in fact anyone - can map their mind, thoughts, inspirations, goals and much more. Give it a whirl and have fun!

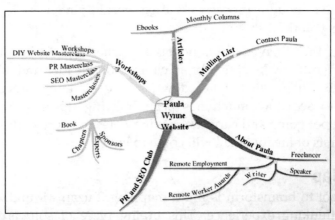

Testing The Market

Research is vital for any project, especially for an online business. There is a multitude of sites out there so you need to know exactly what you are getting into before you rush ahead, spending money on a fancy website, only to find there are several hundred already doing the same thing.

QUICK TEST

- ❑ Write down a target market for your business.
- ❑ Create a simple questionnaire.
- ❑ Aim to get around 20 or 30 responses.
- ❑ Phone the decision maker.
- ❑ Record the results in case you need this later.
- ❑ Only count the definite 'yes' responses – you want at least 50% to be strongly positive to your idea.

THOUGHTFUL

I find it handy to use a personal tape recorder or Dictaphone; it goes pretty much everywhere with me in case I can't make notes. A BlackBerry and other fancy mobiles can also do this.

POSSIBLE QUESTIONS
- ❑ Do you currently buy this product or service?
- ❑ If it were available, would you buy it?
- ❑ How much would you pay for it?
- ❑ What else would affect your decision to buy it?

Research List

Researching your business idea is just the beginning. Create a list of other subjects you need to investigate. Start with a few simple tasks and keep adding to the list as you think of new ones. Here are a few examples to get you going, but come back and list new action points after each chapter or keep a Word document or spreadsheet with all the details.

RESEARCH EXAMPLES
- ❑ Make contacts.
- ❑ You may need to interview experts, depending on your site and your specialty, this could even be professionals.
- ❑ Start meeting and getting to know some of the people who could help you down the line.
- ❑ Check out potential domain names.
- ❑ Research developers for your website – more to come.
- ❑ Check out the competition - what they do best and worst.
- ❑ What are their colours, fonts and designs?
- ❑ What you do better or can do differently? More on this in Branding.
- ❑ Why should your visitors buy from you?
- ❑ What trends, styles and development will you pursue?

Niche

Dictionary.com describes a 'niche' as "a place or position suitable or appropriate for a person or thing and having specific appeal." When we set up Remote Employment there was a need for professional workers to find home based jobs. So our niche not only had specific appeal to *us personally*, but also to our potential users.

At the time there was no reliable website or directory that we could lay our hands on, and so we trawled the web looking for all our keywords only to find loads of 'dodgy' sites and link farms claiming they offered 'genuine' work-from-home jobs.

> *"All sites must evolve or die."*
> Karen Hanton, Toptable

Polly Gowers from Everyclick advises: Find your niche, find out where you customers are hanging out online, find out what keywords they use and then find a way of getting in front of them.

Finding Your Niche

It's really important to find your niche and now is the time to research it. When contemplating your niche, carefully consider the following questions.

KAREN HANTON ON MAKING MISTAKES...

- We all make wrong turns. Anyone who says they don't is probably not being truthful.

- Most important thing is to recognise and accept that something isn't right and fixing it is the easy part. Denial is the enemy!

Ask yourself:

- ❏ What are you passionate about?
- ❏ Are you knowledgeable and skilled on a certain subject?
- ❏ Is your content general or specific?
- ❏ Can you write about broad or narrow topics?

FOR EXAMPLE: you may be a photographer, so what's niche about that? Well, maybe you specialise in underwater photography or newly born babies. If you're a commercial photographer your niche may be shooting scenes such as factory equipment, food or rock concerts.

Above all, you should only 'niche' it up if you love your chosen web concept and you know a lot about it. Don't settle with a topic you're unsure about just because you think it will make money or be a runaway success. Do what you love the most, where your passion will ride waves and your energy will be unstoppable.

Why You, Why Now?

Now take the time to list all the reasons for setting up this fabulous new site; it will help refine your research.

IS IT A NECESSITY AND WHY?

At the time we set up Remote Employment, there was no dedicated port of call to find home based or flexible remote working jobs.

IS THERE A GAP IN THE MARKET?
HOW WILL YOUR SITE FILL THE GAP?

For us there was a clear gap in the market and Remote Employment aimed to fill it with a job board that offered people the first and best site for alternative working.

DEBBIE BIRD ON PLANNING YOUR WEBSITE...

- When planning the structure of your website think bigger than just what you need now.
- Have a vision of where you want to be in 5, 10 and 15 years' time.
- Once you have that vision, start planning how to get there.

WHO WILL BENEFIT AND WHY?

We want to make a difference to people's lives. Everyone who has a flexible work option will enjoy so many benefits. This encompasses parents, carers and generally anyone who wants an alternative way of working. You may have a more specific target market so list the details here.

WHAT WILL IT ACHIEVE & HOW DO YOU INTEND TO DO THIS?

With The Remote Worker Awards we wanted to raise awareness for remote and home working and increase our site traffic. We did this with a huge injection of self driven PR.

WHY ARE YOU THE BEST PERSON TO DO THIS?

We were the first and as such we became industry experts on the topic of remote working. As a result, we are often called upon by the media to comment on remote and home working.

Exit Route

No, it's not a roadie film or anything similar. An exit strategy, also known as exit route, is just what it says on the tin. It is a plan for exiting the business or company, either due to an unsuitable situation or by forward planning, which is why I am mentioning it now.

You may want to maintain a long running family business in a cottage industry and keep it that way. No problem with that. Or you may have plans to make a mint and then let someone else take over when the time is right to sell. This is where your exit plan comes in handy.

Jo Haigh, from *fds* and MGR advises that you plan your exit the day you start your business. In other words, always have in mind what your business should look like to potential investors to get the best value possible. Having a great management team and a strong brand are steps in the right direction.

KAREN HANTON ON MANAGEMENT STRATEGIES...

✓ It is good to have a high profile shareholder.

✓ If you have a good proposition, it shouldn't be too hard to interest somebody relevant to your audience in return for a small share.

Most entrepreneurs set up a Strategic Management Team with a clear exit plan for some point in the future. Investors will be interested in this, as it shows them a way that they can recoup any money they invest in your business. The most common exit route is selling the business to someone else. And if you have an investor, they get a return on their investment once the sale is complete.

Deciding to exit, or not, doesn't make or break you as an entrepreneur, it just decides the future outcome of your online business. Don't stress over this now if you hadn't even considered this option. Just let it sit in your bubbling pot and see what happens when you finish this book. Even then, you don't have to make a decision until you know what is best for you and the business. If you plan to build the business with a clear exit route in place then remember to make notes in your SWOT analysis.

Management Team

Jo describes a Non-Executive Director (NED) as a member of the Board of Directors who form part of the executive management team, but may not be an employee of the company. Working with an NED should strengthen your management team (remember to explore this in your SWOT Analysis), especially if they are an industry expert and you are not. It could be a good idea to make contact with possible NEDs at an early stage of your planning. Think carefully about the essential skills you need yet don't have and interview or select NEDs based on this list.

Consider someone with experience in the areas where you and your team are possibly weak. You could also look for a few people who will complement your business and use their skills and experience to reinforce your SWOTs. You may want to offer them a Sweat Equity, which is a share (preferably small) in your business in return for their sweat … err, their help and advice.

Jo suggests that you choose only those people who are better than you in whatever area you feel deficient and make sure you like them! You need to have a clear understanding of what you want from them and what they can do for you, and then communicate this to them so both parties have full understanding of the agreement.

"Learn to delegate. You can't possibly do everything yourself. Find other specialists that can do certain things better than you."

Polly Gowers, Everyclick

Jo also advises that you have clearly defined rules of engagement. What happens if they leave or you want them to leave? Lastly, on the subject of Non Executives, Jo believes that you should not mix up consultancy with NED roles. Instead, have agreed director's fees; a contract for services should you not get an NED involved in your business.

Mentor

Dictionary.com tells us that a mentor is a wise and trusted teacher or an influential sponsor and supporter. Do yourself the biggest favour and find one of these wise owls by asking someone you respect. Or make contact with industry experts through people you meet or know. Networking is a perfect way to meet possible NEDs and mentors.

Imagine winning a mentor who is one of the most successful woman entrepreneurs in the UK! I did! Let me tell you, I still pinch myself. I was awarded Karen Darby as my mentor in the FreshIdeas Events Award.

We've had the greatest fun, from her flipping pancakes - and serving them with ice cream at our meetings - to fishing frogs out of her pond for an exhibition!

Aside from the good laughs, Karen has given me bucket loads of inspiration and her confidence in my business concept has been a huge boost. Every time I see her (even if it's only for a pub lunch or coffee) I walk away buzzing with excitement and creative thoughts whirring in every direction.

Working with a mentor may initiate imaginative thinking, create new ideas for long term strategies and help you to evolve your business or website over time. Karen has done all this for me and more.

WHY A MENTOR?

A mentor may offer a long term commitment and a vested interest in you and your business's future. The mentor could be where you aspire to be and they may even come gift wrapped with the influence and contacts you need.

A GOOD MENTOR

- Willingness to share their experience
- Constructive feedback or criticism
- Share their brain power
- Your ideal role model
- Similar backgrounds
- Good sense of humour
- Listening skills
- Ability to discuss wide range of issues
- Aspiration to bring about change
- Positive upbeat attitude
- Open to learning from you

FINDING A MENTOR

Ask at your network events or within other organisations to see if there's a mentoring programme you can join. Surf the net as well, as there are various websites on mentoring.

To find someone, identify a person you admire and respect. Go back and look at your goals and see the notes you made on your management team and decide what characteristics you're seeking in a mentor. Do some research on people you'd like to work with; you can even use LinkedIn to find people you have seen speak at seminars or functions. First, approach them for a link or connection before you cram them with requests to give up their time for you.

FIND A MENTOR

✓ Don't be afraid to ask someone to be your mentor, they can only say 'No.' Nothing lost, experience gained.

✓ Dust yourself down and try again. And keep trying until you find someone who will help you, support you and guide you through the ups and downs.

APPROACHING A MENTOR

When you approach your wise owl, go slowly and don't bombard a possible mentor; it could make them say NO! Test the waters by a simple request for their advice on a particular challenge that you know will be their forté. Or make a direct request. Be open, honest, realistic and enthusiastic.

Another way is to buy them a coffee or splash out and do lunch. If you both feel good afterwards, there is probably a basis for a mentorship. Don't forget to thank them for their time, even if the idea of mentoring is going nowhere.

When you have their trust, tell them your intentions and request a trial mentoring period. That way it gives them an opt-out if they feel that they won't be able to help you and vice versa.

YOU AS A MENTEE

You should show your potential mentor trustworthiness and confidentiality. Agree from the start how things will work and how you will communicate. Decide on boundaries together and clarify time commitments and expectations.

JO HAIGH ADVISES MENTEES...
- ✓ Don't ask too much
- ✓ Do what you have agreed
- ✓ Stick to time tables
- ✓ Open your mind - you will learn loads!

There are thousands of networking groups where you could scout for your mentor. Some of them even pair mentees and mentors, such as FreshIdeas Events where I saw the competition, applied and was awarded Karen as my mentor. Jackie Brennan, from FreshIdeas Events, is an excellent mentor matcher and has advised on both mentor and mentee topics. Check out Jackie's mentoring program at www.freshideasevents.com/services.asp.

What a ride! You may not be flipping pancakes or fishing for pond life, but the inspiration and motivation, as well as good common business sense, will set you on fire and make you aspire to be as successful as they are. Don't just get a Mentor, get one today!

Summary

Today's topics and tasks are the foundations of your new website. Prepping up and setting objectives at this stage will pay off later on.

We set short and long term goals, objectives and SMART goals for your site to steer you in the right direction. As you venture on your quest to ensure online success for your website, analysing your strengths and weaknesses will help you recognise the opportunities that lie ahead of you. We discussed options for managing your online business and watching out for competitors.

Brainstorm all possible avenues of research so you get all the 'must do' tasks out of the way because we are now heading into some pretty exciting stuff. We've had some fun today and we've done some serious soul searching to determine all that needs to be done in planning your new online business.

Checklist

- ❏ Naming your site
- ❏ SWOT analysis
- ❏ Brainstorm
- ❏ Create an iMind Map
- ❏ Research list
- ❏ Set SMART goals

- ❏ Why me, why now?
- ❏ Consider your exit route
- ❏ Management team
- ❏ Non Executive Director
- ❏ Potential mentors
- ❏ Competitive analysis

Day 2: Branding

Build Your Brand

The topic we cover today is one of my favourites; I love watching a brand take seed, then grow and prosper. In particular, I enjoy the innovative process of creating something from nothing and then branding it with colours, themes, fonts, styles, layouts and everything else that forms a recognisable and profitable online venture.

We'll discuss how to brand your website, how to punch above your weight and look 'the business'. Let's get going!

What Is A Brand?

In Philip Kotler's book, *Principles of Marketing*, he describes a brand as: "a name, a term, sign, symbol or design or a combination of these, intended to identify the goods or services of one seller or group of sellers and to differentiate them from those of competitors."

He goes on to explain that a brand image is the set of beliefs that consumers hold about a particular brand. Philip's book is an excellent study of brand marketing and there are plenty of others.

Brand and Deliver

Now that you have a definite idea for your business, you will need to decide on certain aspects of branding. Your brand will most likely be determined by your audience, either business clients (B2B) or consumer visitors (B2C).

With Remote Employment we have both. Our visitors are primarily consumers, who are working professional candidates or job seekers. We also attract employers, agencies and companies that would post jobs, so we considered both audiences when we determined our brand. Like us, you will want to ensure your site is not too busy with cheap clip art or graphic images, it should be easy to navigate and should look professional.

Create an impression that is suitable for your market and the position you want to fill within it. Should your site look clean and smart? Or busy and full? Should it be young and modern or traditional and conventional? Do you want to portray an image of high luxury or good value? The look and feel of these options will be different and guided by your business concept as well as the target audience you aim to attract.

> *"The Mumsnetters are our brand –*
> *often their controversial conversations are*
> *picked up by the press and this attention has*
> *certainly helped to grow the brand."*
> Carrie Longton, Mumsnet

The best looking sites are often clean and simple with a light and airy feel and a spacious design. Avoid heavy and dark backgrounds and overuse of flashy objects. It jars and gets on most people's nerves. Even with fast speed broadband, they also take so long to download and often people give up before they find the solution you're offering.

A VISUAL IDENTITY

Marketers use branding to make people sit up and take notice. They want people to know their company and their product or service from memory.

Aim to get them to trust you more than they trust your competitors. They should want to come back to your online business before thinking of any others.

Your Website Brand

When designing your brand, take into account even the little things that matter such as making sure your logo is visible on all your pages. Your logo brands the whole site with your company's image.

HERE ARE SOME IMPORTANT BRAND POINTS

- Most sites are branded in the header and footer area.
- If you have a slogan or catch phrase, use it with your logo because it helps to reinforce your key message. Don't think that having this across the whole site will be over the top, it won't. Instead, repeated exposure through this and other methods is vital to developing a successful brand.
- Be sure to keep all your design elements the same from page to page and from marketing material to marketing campaign.
- A consistent brand gives a powerful stamp of credibility to your online business.
- All of your marketing material should reflect a consistent image and message of your online business.
- What colour schemes will you use and why?
- Your colour scheme and layout should also be recognised across your site.
- Consider which particular colours will go with your brand and research them.
- Decide if you are B2B (business to business), B2C (business to consumer), or both.
- Explore your website's personality and what 'language' to use.
- Come up with ways to punch above your weight so you can look bigger than you are – this helps to be classed as a 'player' or expert in your field.

MAX BENSON, MBE ON SETTING UP THE EVERYWOMAN BRAND...

"We involved everyone who touched our business in our branding process. We asked our teams, suppliers and customers to tell us how they saw us."

A NOTE ON COLOUR SCHEMES

If you really want to make an impact, try Googling 'colour schemes', 'colour meanings' or 'colour explanation'. There are many sites that are dedicated to informing you about the emotional and psychological effects that colours have on humans. It not only makes interesting reading, but you can build themes based on colour combinations that really match you and your audience.

Also Google 'colour matching' for a variety of sites that will help to match the colour of your choice with other complimentary colours.

There are many colour matching sites, but I found www.hypergurl.com/colormatch.php and www.knorrpage.de/colormatch.html, to have useful colour wheels.

Pink and Fluffy

Mumsnet set out to have a certain tone – not 'pink and fluffy', but 'realistic and witty', 'modern and democratic'.

FAVICON

1. Use a Favicon (those small icons in the browser's bookmarks) to brand your site and increase prominence.

2. Upload your logo and get an instant Favicon at http://tools.dynamicdrive.com/favicon

3. Follow Dynamic Drive's instructions to insert your shiny new Favicon into your site.

They also wanted to be empathetic, helpful and down to earth. They've attracted a bunch of educated and opinionated members whose daily acts of kindness and generosity make Mumsnet what it is – and they are very proud of that.

Favicon

A Favicon is short for favourite icon and is that itsy, bitsy, tiny logo seen on branded sites beside the URL domain name.

There's a small, 16x16 pixel image that is shown inside the browser's location bar and bookmark menu when your site is found. It's ideally used to brand your site and increase its prominence in your visitor's bookmark menu. There are several sites that you can use to generate your own Favicon. Just Google 'favicon generator' and check out the range available to you. Be sure to test a few though as some of them don't produce good quality. The one that gave me a clear image was the first one on the list of links below.

LINKS

- www.favicon.co.uk
- www.favicon.cc
- http://tools.dynamicdrive.com/favicon
- www.favicongenerator.com

Look 'The Business'

To ensure your site communicates who you are, what product you feature or which service you offer, and what your brand promises, be consistent in design, logo and page content.

CORPORATE PERSONALITY

Think about your corporate personality. Will it be formal or fun? If you have a technical product or service, you can take on a techie persona. If you are providing a business service, your corporate personality will be formal and if you offer consumer merchandise you will match the site's personality to the product range and intended customers.

We decided to retain a certain amount of formality as we wanted to look professional, but we also have fun. Whichever you choose, your look and feel must communicate your brand both visually and verbally.

COLOUR EFFECTS

You will see from the Remote Employment and The Remote Worker Awards sites that we have used effective branding techniques.

Visitors often comment that our site is considered to be clean and professional with lots of white space. It reflects personality, yet speaks to both B2B and B2C audiences.

Punch Above Your Weight

Visitors to our site constantly comment on the distinct 'feel' we created. The bright theme and fresh colouring, alongside easy navigation and an uncluttered design, speaks for itself.

We used green for several reasons, mostly because it is a lovely serene and calming colour and its eco-friendly symbolism is also appropriate.

Most people believe that there is a large corporate organisation behind our site. We use our brand to punch above our weight so we don't come across as a home business. Only when you browse through our pages on the 'Co Founders' and 'Meet The Team' do you realise that we are a small business. Now, let's work on getting *you* to look the business.

Research Brands

While you need to research your target market, your competitors' sites and your industry's leading brands, one of the keys to your success is to analyse your audience. You need to know who your visitors are and what they expect from you. Find out if they are internet savvy or if they require basic steps to get through your site.

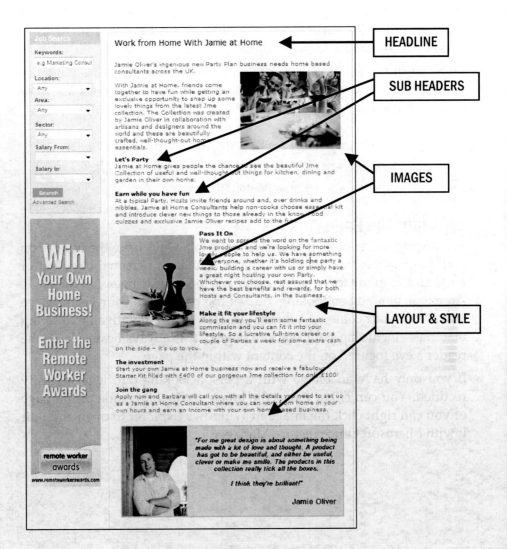

HEADLINE

SUB HEADERS

IMAGES

LAYOUT & STYLE

White Space

If you have a quick peek at both Remote Employment and The Remote Worker Awards, you will see that we have made good use of 'White Space'. When looking around at various sites to get some ideas for your brand, notice which ones make use of this basic, yet simple and highly effective route to professional branding.

By all means, use colour, images and content, but to create a quality site that looks like the top designers and branding agencies have created it, use plenty of white space!

"Partnerships can be useful for brand awareness, even if they don't make you money as such."

Karen Hanton, Toptable

Look Into The Page

A branding secret often not discussed, is to always have the images on your page facing *into* the page. This is actually a personal bug bear of mine and so many top websites still have people facing *out* of the page. An image of a person looking 'out' of the page takes your visitor's eye away from your content. A minor issue, I know, but with all marketing material – including your website pages - it is always best to keep the reader's eye focused on the content within the page.

If you only have an image with a person looking out, it is so easily rectified. You can either move the image to the other side of the page or you can right click the image in Windows Explorer to open and edit it with Microsoft Office Picture Manager.

Here's how you can flip an image in Picture Manager.

1. Click on 'Edit Picture'
2. This opens a sidebar, click on 'rotate and flip'
3. This opens a new sidebar, click 'flip horizontal'
4. The image now faces the other way

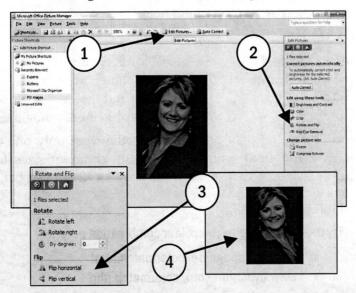

Page Layout Golden Rules

- Use sub headings
- Use bullets
- Break up paragraphs
- Use web fonts: Arial, Times New Roman, Verdana
- Be clear about your page goals
- Update little and often - in bite size chunks
- Ensure images face into the page

FREE FONTS

Font Space offers you a mammoth range of free fonts for your logo and brand: www.fontspace.com

Branding Brief

Create a briefing document to determine how the company brand should be used. Large corporate companies spend a vast fortune on their brand documentation and, for obvious reasons, only give certain people the right to manage it. I advise you do the same, but on a smaller scale. Draw up a simple Word document starting with your logo at the top, company name and brand objectives.

Take this a step further and decide on important criteria such as:

- Header font and size (H1)
- Sub header font and size (H2 – H5)
- Body font and size

- Colour Schemes
- Complimentary colours
- Fonts and their sizes
- Logo placement guidelines

You should consider using only one font or at the most only one or two similar fonts throughout your website, with different sizes for headers, sub headers and body text. Verdana size 10 – 12 is a safe bet.

MATCHING COLOURS

Try these sites to give you colour combination palettes:

- www.knorrpage.de/colormatch.html
- www.hypergurl.com/colormatch.php

Choosing Fonts

Stick to certain fonts to ensure legibility on your website. Clare Medden believes that it is safest sticking to the following font families:

Sans-Serif Fonts

- Arial
- Helvetica
- Tahoma
- Verdana

Serif Fonts

- Century Schoolbook
- Georgia
- Liberation Serif
- Times New Roman

Remember that many fonts have their copyrights owned by the operating system (Microsoft, Apple etc). So ask your developer to build using these lists of fonts to ensure a viewer will see the site in a close alternative, if they do not have the specified font on their system.

Clare also recommends going for the Verdana or Arial lists, as they are the only two sans-serif fonts distributed with Windows, Apple and Linux systems. More information on installed fonts can be found here: www.codestyle.org/css/font-family/sampler-CombinedResults.shtml

IN A NUTSHELL
Be sure to use easy to read fonts that all browsers can see and read. Once you have decided what they will be, stick to them rigorously and don't deviate from them.

Branding Awareness
There are several different ways you should continue to filter your 'website image' through to your audience, all of which will maintain your brand awareness. Try implementing some of these suggestions:

YOUR DOMAIN
Wherever possible use your domain name as your brand. Show it off on all your business stationery and marketing material.

> **FOR EXAMPLE:** when we started up we called ourselves RemotEmployment.com to reinforce our web presence.

THANK YOU AND COME AGAIN
If you have any form pages, such as application forms, contact us, information requests or subscription forms that need completing, use the final page as a way to thank your visitors with your logo and thank you message. Also, use this page to highlight any promotional links.

 SEO (Search Engine Optimisation) is the process of improving your ranking in search engine results.

E-SHOTS OR E-NEWS
Set up and use a mailing list to drive your domain name and brand. If possible, create a header and footer that is the same as the one on your site and use this consistently to either sell or give your list members topics of interest.

ARTICLES

The demand for good quality content is a top priority on all web owners' to do lists, so make it easy to get your articles published on other sites with relevant content.

At the bottom of the article suggest that anyone can use the content if they credit your name, website and provide a link back to the article on a specific web page. Not only will this help you build incoming links, you also get the free publicity thrown in (learn about SEO in my 2nd book, *Pimp My Site*).

E-SIGNATURE

Carry your brand and key message on through your emails and keep it neatly in your signature. More on this in a minute.

AUTO RESPONDERS

The idea is that they can provide an automated email reply 24/7 and you don't have to be on hand to do a thing, except set them up in the first place. Use them to send free reports, articles, links and to keep your brand and domain in full view.

I am the recipient of some auto responders and they do sometimes work for me, but they can also be intrusive if they don't stop coming, so use them wisely. Before sending out too many automated emails, think about how you would feel if you were on the other end.

E-BOOKS

E-books are a good way to send your brand around the world via your visitors' distribution tools. If someone likes your downloaded E-book and thinks friends or colleagues should get a copy, it is forwarded on without you even knowing. That's viral marketing at its best. Learn how to create an E-book in *Pimp My Site*.

Email Signature

Everyone who reads your email will be exposed to your consistent branding. Use your logo, the same font and colour scheme, your tagline or slogan and, of course, your website link. You can also show off your awards and carry all your social media links. Some may say that your signature is too long if you cram in all your social media links but this is a personal preference.

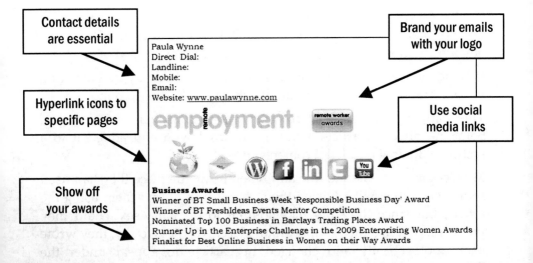

Contact details are essential

Brand your emails with your logo

Hyperlink icons to specific pages

Use social media links

Show off your awards

SET UP AN EMAIL SIGNATURE

Take these easy steps to set up a signature in Outlook:

1. Go to Tools > Options > Format Mail Format > Signatures.
2. Click on the 'new' button and save the name of the signature.
3. You then have the choice to insert text, images and link your website as well as the various social media links. You can either insert icons or links to show your website and social media links.
4. Once you have created your text, highlight the word you want linked, copy the link, click the link button and paste the link into the box. This way your links will be live in your email signature and people can click directly to your site.

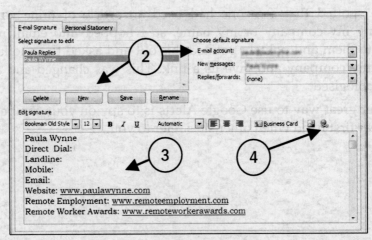

Google Alerts

Did you know that you can set up Google Alerts to be notified when any information containing your name or company is used online?

If someone has posted information about you that may be damaging to your brand contact them immediately and ask them to remove it.

This happened to me, but it wasn't damaging, just embarrassing. Someone lifted an article about an award I won and added it to a section of their site called 'Women and Sex'.

My Google Alert 'alerted' me and when I saw the piece they had used I sent them an email advising them that I didn't mind them using the article, but since the story had nothing to do with 'sex' could they please place it in a more appropriate place. Needless to say, they wrote back apologetically and changed my article to appear under the 'Women and Careers' section instead.

If something like that happens to you, don't get ticked off. Instead consider that you are getting publicity in front of their visitors and hopefully they will click to your site, which is a great way to build your traffic. So, just write a polite email asking for changes to be made.

Also, be aware of your articles being used without your name being credited.

> **FOR EXAMPLE:** When I send out a Press Release or article, I always set up a Google Alert and then I see where the release or article is being used.

I once spotted that someone had used an article of mine without crediting my company or my name, so I hopped into email mode, wrote to them and politely pointed this out and asked them to kindly credit my company and give us a link. This was changed and again they apologised.

Another great way to use Google Alerts is to spy on your competitors and hear first hand when other sites refer to you.

IN A NUTSHELL

See where your articles are used and check references to your name and your company.

You can even set Google Alerts up with your keywords to see how others are using those keywords, although this is a cumbersome task to trawl through each day. Been there, done that!

Set Up A Google Account

There are many products available to you under one Google Account. If you don't have a Google Account yet then set one up now. You will be able to link your Google Analytics (coming later on) with Blogger, YouTube and all the other nifty tools on Google's smorgasbord. As we go through each section you will learn more about your Google Account and it will slowly come to life right under your fingertips.

How To Set Up Google Alerts

Take these easy steps to set up a Google Alert, which can be daily, weekly or as-it-happens. They update you with the latest relevant results based on your choice of keywords in the alert.

STEP BY STEP GUIDE

1. Go to www.google.com

2. Set up new account

3. Enter all your details.

4. Google then sends an email to verify you exist

5. Choose which products you want to include and set each of them up individually. Then set up a Google Alert with your name or company as shown in this screenshot.

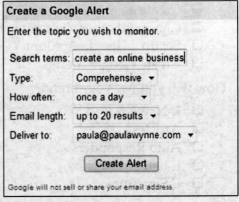

COOL WAYS TO USE ALERTS

- Monitoring a news story
- Keeping up to date on your competitors or your industry
- Following your favourite celebrity or event
- Keeping tabs on a sports team
- Find out what competitors are up to
- Manage your alerts by adding more or deleting old ones

Summary

Today we set about planting your branding seeds so you can watch it grow over the chapters in this book. Essentially, today was all about ensuring style, layout and creating a recognisable and trusted brand.

I hope you enjoyed the process of creating your brand's colours, themes, fonts, styles, layouts and design. Above all, I really look forward to you punching above your weight and looking the business in years to come.

Checklist

What will be your brand?

- ❑ How will it be communicated to your audience?
- ❑ Create a Favicon
- ❑ Check out other site's navigation
- ❑ Set up a Google Account
- ❑ Create Google Alerts

How will you use your brand?

- ❑ E-News
- ❑ Articles
- ❑ Auto Responders
- ❑ E-books
- ❑ E-Signature

Day 3: Navigation

Navigate Your Site

Now that you've established your brand and explored ways to use it effectively, let's discuss your website navigation.

I have broken this down into different topics so, before we go into the details of how to set up your website's navigation, let's first cover how you will manage this navigation and define the various terms that are used to describe the 'innards' of your website.

CMS: Content Management System

A CMS is software or an 'admin' area for managing your website content, thus known as a Content Management System.

A CMS is the engine that allows you to manage the site, add content and gives you control 24/7. It also makes life easier and is way, way cheaper than having to constantly ask your developer to add content for you. That is just not an option!

POLLY GOWERS ON BRANDING...

- **Everyclick is an online brand.**
- **One of our straplines was 'Give your mouth a heart'.**
- **To bring the brand to life we had two 8ft blue mice who wandered around doing acts of kindness and appearing at Charity Events.**

Today, most websites are developed for you to log in and manage your 'front end' (what people see) by making changes to the 'back end' (your admin or CMS).

If you are developing a site with a development company then insist on having your own bespoke admin section so you have complete control of your site.

This admin should enable you to control page content, your banners, layout, navigation and page order. From a long term and short term view this is definitely the way to go.

WYSIWYG

Most CMS provide an editing tool which has a 'what you see is what you get' interface. This type of editor is fondly known as WYSIWYG (pronounced wizzie-wig). This makes editing your pages flexible and easy, however it can cause more problems than it solves, especially in terms of web standards and new users not understanding web design.

Clare Medden suggests that non-experienced users of a WYSIWYG interface could end up 'trashing' a site's design, especially on sites that have more than one administrator. One of the key aspects of good web design is keeping your content and design totally separate.

COLOURING YOUR SITE

Imagine you write an article, and decide to make the headline orange, which you think goes nicely with the yellow colour scheme of your site. A year later, when you update the design to a different colour, you have to go through and change every article that you coloured orange. A laborious and tedious task. If you did it using Cascading Style Sheets (CSS) you would simply change one colour value in a separate file, and it would be reflected on your entire site instantly.

 Wikipedia defines Cascading Style Sheets (CSS) as a Style Sheet Language used to describe the presentation, the look and formatting, such as the layout, colours and fonts, of a web page.

Understanding Web Pages

Pages are called different things by different people or experts. Understanding these terms will help you to build and develop your site efficiently and professionally. A grasp of the terms and how best to develop certain types of pages will be important as you become a little more ambitious with your website's development.

Sitemap

A Sitemap enables your website to quickly show search engines which URLs (the individual address of each of your web pages) are available for crawling and indexing. Wikipedia describes this as XML (code readable by search engines). It also shows the pages of your site which may not be visible through your navigation, or where content such as 'Flash' (used for animations and interactive features), is used.

Parents

Parents are the main navigation elements you see on most sites. They are also known as 'categories' and 'primary links' in some CMS systems.

> **FOR EXAMPLE:** a 'Parent' on Remote Worker Awards would be 'Enter' and 'Judges'. Parents are generally used as the main section pages.

Children

Don't lose your children! 'Children' or 'secondary links' are pages that lead off the 'Parent' page. In this Remote Worker Awards example you will see that each 'Award Category and Judge' has their own page stemming from the Parent.

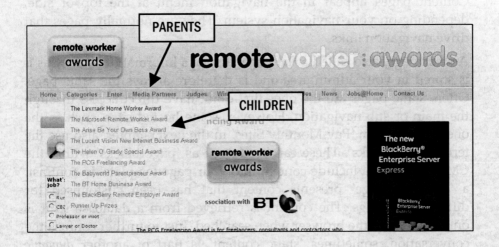

Page Rank

Most systems give you the ability to rank or order your pages in your navigation map or menu. This is particularly handy to prioritise content pages in order of importance and relevance to your visitors. Some systems such as Drupal call this 'page weight'.

Orphans

As the name suggests, these pages are normally pages that have somehow lost their parents. Most commonly, this is when you have inadvertently removed their parent page.

Believe me, it happens, so do be aware of this if you have a content managed system. I encountered this problem when we were setting up the Remote Worker Awards site and had to wait a week before our developer could go into the HTML code, find the parents and reinstate them. A costly error! Some developers also consider orphans to be pages that don't belong to anyone in particular. They are also called 'stand alone' pages.

> FOR EXAMPLE: they could be your terms and conditions page or other generic pages that are not specific to a certain area but still essential to your website.

Content, Static and Dynamic Pages

Content pages appear in the navigation menu at the top or side, depending on your navigation system. They are normally pages that drive navigation links.

A static page, also called a flat page, displays information exactly as it is stored in your admin area and is therefore always the same page. Often, static pages are the ones that don't have direct access through the main or sub navigation. However, some hosted sites, such as the ones described in 'Pay Monthly Sites' in the next chapter, also use the term 'static blocks'. These can be classed as 'page blocks' within the CMS that let you include content into your page template. In contrast, a 'dynamic page' presents content that has been customised for different viewings. The content is retrieved from a database so it is only on view to the browser when searched. Just to further confuse the conversation, sometimes 'static content' is part of another *dynamic* page, such as the panels used on Pimp My Site Club's home page to divide up content. Sometimes it is a whole page in its own right.

An example of this is when you may have a page that normally you wouldn't get access to, such as a mailing list form page that is hard-coded by your developer. Yet you need to be in control of that page's text and so your developer has given you access to the text just above or below the form on the page.

This mailing page on the Remote Worker Awards has two parts; a dynamic text area above with a hard-coded form below.

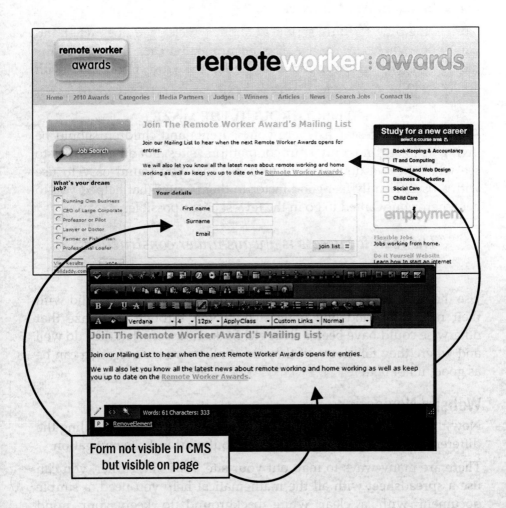

Form not visible in CMS but visible on page

I know your head must be swimming with these different terms and what they all mean, but this will get clearer after we have covered Free Websites and Hosted Websites. You can also find in-depth explanations in Google or Wikipedia.

BRINGING THE FAMILY TOGETHER

Going back to the start of your navigation, you can now bring the whole fan-damily together. The old fashioned way to do this could be to lay out postcards on the floor. You can use one postcard for each section which is then numbered by area. Or you can use a superfast digital format in Word or Excel.

Now is the time to think seriously about which page does what and what goes where. In a sense, it is ensuring that each member of the family is living in the right area, under the correct roof and with accurate clothing.

STEER THROUGH THE MAZE

A good way to research where your parents and children should be 'living' is to surf not only your competitors' sites, but all good sites to see what they've done. Check websites that you found easy to use with a user-friendly feel-good factor to them - sites that helped you to get where you wanted to go in the fewest clicks possible.

"The road to success is always under construction."
Anonymous

Use the time now to go back and see what these 'good sites' did with their navigation and how they steered you through the maze that otherwise could have been a struggle. Make notes of what they do well and where they fall down, if they do at all, so your navigation can be as good, if not better.

Website Navigation

Now that you've identified all the funny names you will be calling the different pages on your site, let's thrash out your website navigation.

There are many ways to map out your site. As I said earlier, you can use a spreadsheet with all the mathematical help you need, a simple document with a clear white background to keep your mind uncluttered or even Microsoft's One Note, which has both the clear background and the use of tabs.

Some might prefer the old card system by laying out post cards on a table or even the floor, writing the main headings on them and then shuffling them into a map system until you have found the ideal chart.

Essentially, you should focus on organisation of the content. Your site will be divided into sections according to user needs and expectations.

NAVIGATION BRIEF

From the list below make notes about your navigation which will form your navigation brief.

This is the document you will provide to a developer if you are creating a bespoke site. Some instant sites also create semi bespoke sites with your navigation brief, so keep it handy. You may want to print it off and have a play around with it while you're on the bus or train. A good way to use wasted time on public transport to your advantage!

Navigation Map

Break your website down into sections and think of it as a touring map. If you were travelling abroad in a campervan you will have looked at the areas and tourist spots you want to visit.

We'll do something similar with your navigation map in order to outline exactly what your site should have for visitors.

First, let's think about some of your favourite sites. Go to them and you should be able to find what you're looking for in a matter of seconds; if you can't you'll probably leave. The same goes for your web pages. Your site must be easy to navigate!

Don't let your viewers leave without finding what they came for. Your home page is your starting point. Most visitors come in here and leave from here so it is the most important page.

Although you can get found and you *do* want to get found through other pages, your home page is an important starting point. When we discuss SEO and Page Optimisation in *Pimp My Site*, you'll see that it's just as important to get found through any and all of your *own* pages.

So with your navigation map, you need to decide exactly what you want to achieve and revisit your goals to remind yourself of your targets. If you are running an online shop you need to show this and feature your most popular or bestselling products right up front. If you want visitors to buy a particular item or offer then make *that* the first thing they see.

Your home page should preferably not have other sections coming off it. However, this is personal taste. Most sites don't do this, as they want to lead visitors in a particular direction, but it's your choice and also depends on the web platform and CMS (Content Management System) you end up using.

Ensure that your home page features the most important details, such as your USP, what's different and better about your business, and your site's key message – what it does, who it's for, who it benefits – and all of this in one or two paragraphs. You can also divide up content into panels or blocks such as Remote Employment and Pimp My Site Club.

Map It Out

Map out a brief according to the following points...

CONTACT IS KEY

Your contact page should provide all your contact details. You should make it easy for people to get hold of you, even if you are a cyber business that doesn't always need to see clients or customers. Place your phone number on all your pages and have a map and directions if you need to direct people to your premises. Due to spammers I would recommend that you use a contact form for people to get hold of you by email. Also, if you do wish to show your email address, in case people want to email direct, then spell out the words, even the word 'at' and the 'dot com' to prevent people easily harvesting your email address using automated software and then sending you spam.

> **FOR EXAMPLE:** I use 'paula at paula wynne dot com' or 'paula at remote employment dot com'. This helps to prevent your email being caught in a spammer's net and you getting tons of nonsense, unless you happen to need Viagra!

LEFT, RIGHT OR ON TOP

There are several different navigation systems to use and, depending on the developer or software, you will find some have a left side menu or tabs at the top. And others navigate from both. These are often classed as categories, blocks or primary links.

SEEK AND YOU SHALL FIND

If you have a range of products, give your visitors an easy ride by providing a search box. The quicker they can find what they are looking for on your site, the more likely they are to return again and again and do business with you.

ABOUT US

This is a great way of including all the relevant aspects about your online business, yourself and your team. If you are struggling with space to fit a minimum amount of main navigation headings, at a push you could use this page to show your contact details, but I strongly recommend a 'Contact Us' page. Most people today won't deal with a company that they can't contact in some way. I don't!

TELL A FRIEND

Use your visitors as mini marketing tools; add a page where they can tell their friends and family how wonderful your site is.

MAILING LIST

Consider the option of adding a mailing list. A mailing list gives you the chance to stay in touch and tell your fans about the great new features and content you've added to your site.

COPY CAT

Many sites feel they need to include a copyright statement at the bottom of the page. This is not essential, but good to have if you're concerned about people stealing your content.

TERMS AND CONDITIONS

If you are dealing with a member sign up area, shopping trolleys and other aspects of e-commerce, certain issues may come back and bite you so it is important to show your terms and conditions.

Some people say you may never use them and, let's be honest, we all just tick the box without even glancing at the terms. But then, there are some diligent people who avidly read Ts and Cs like bedtime reading.

PRIVACY POLICY

Your privacy policy should clearly state how you treat and protect your customers' information. It's essential that your policy is easy to find on your website, usually linked from your homepage or in the footer of your site.

When we set up Remote Employment we had a legal eagle go through our Privacy Policy, but if you don't want to incur legal costs, you can draw one up yourself. Browse the web for different documents readily available to help you set up your privacy policy.

PayPal suggests that a typical privacy policy should include:

- What personally identifiable customer information you collect
- How the information is used
- With whom you share and do not share this information
- What choices are available to your customers regarding collection, use and distribution of the information
- The choices available to your customers regarding communication from you – email, direct mail, etc.
- The kind of security procedures in place to protect the loss, misuse, or alteration of information under your control
- How your customers can correct any inaccuracies in the information
- For simplicity, it is recommended you confirm clearly whether or not you intend to store or currently store financial details (credit or debit card numbers)

Here is an example, using PayPal's privacy policy:
https://cms.paypal.com/uk/cgi-bin/marketingweb?cmd=_render-content&content_ID=ua/Privacy_full&locale.x=en_GB

KEEP IT SIMPLE

Clare Medden from Medden Website Design advises keeping your navigation simple and no more than 7 items in one menu, or users won't bother reading them.

She suggests that you organise it into logical categories. Assume your visitors are mindless morons who will not stop to work out your sections. Don't make them think, make it blindingly obvious. Design it for a kiddie and you won't confuse your visitors.

Navigation Rules

Use these top rules to develop a simple and consistent navigation map:

- Think and plan pages in a logical order
- Write out a few simple navigations to get into the swing of things and see how it works
- Check other sites for the best and worst navigation maps
- Keep your 'Calls to Action' visible and easy to find
- Links must be clear as well as the words you use to link
- Images that the user clicks on must be concise and relevant to the information they are leading to
- 5 – 8 main headings are ideal, more can be cluttered
- Keep the text headings short and simple
- Navigation buttons, branding graphics and logos must be in the same place on all of your site pages
- Graphics and images increase the download time so avoid over use of these for navigation
- Ensure it is easy to find info or your visitors will bounce away
- A site map and a search box will help if they get stuck
- Use quick links as locators for content
- Use hyperlinks in your text, carefully sprinkled with keywords (more on this in *Pimp My Site*) to provide easy access to related pages
- When you put yourself in your visitors' shoes, try to anticipate what information they will need next and ensure that your navigation flows easily from page to page
- Use the 'three click rule', which is exactly that – three quick and easy clicks to get to any important page on your site. I know this is not always possible, but keep it in mind to get as few clicks as possible to important areas
- Use your postcard system or produce a diagram that shows the structure and logic behind the content, presentation and navigation
- Start with a skeleton of the main areas, building up your stick figure with pages of content. This is easily changed as you research and muse more on your navigation map
- Consider using an iMind Map for your navigation, go back and look at my example under brainstorming

- Large sites use breadcrumbs
- Include a news page or media room – more on this in the PR chapter in *Pimp My Site*
- Find resources and navigation templates on Pimp My Site Club

Breadcrumbs

A breadcrumb, or a 'breadcrumb trail', is a navigation path used to give visitors a way to keep track of where they are within your website.

Think Hansel and Gretel and the crumbs they left in the popular fairytale. They normally appear horizontally across the top of a web page and enable a user to find their way back through the maze of pages.

Breadcrumbs aren't generally used in a template site and, if you have a small site, they won't be necessary as most surfers use the back button anyway. However, on large sites with thousands of complex pages, they are crucial. If you intend to create a fancy site with the help of a developer, they can advise you on how to use breadcrumb categories in conjunction with your main navigation.

The last time I looked, Remote Employment had 7,501 pages and counting so you can imagine why a breadcrumb trail comes in handy.

The Remote Employment illustration shown here, gives you an idea of how your visitors can find their way back home.

The example above follows this crumbly trail: Home > My Profile > Candidates > Work From Home Articles > How to Set Up a Home Office

If you want to implement this, make a note of it so you can ask your software provider or developer if they can toss a few breadcrumbs your way.

Navigation Map Example

For my own site, which was only designed when I started writing this book, I had initially chosen the following navigation:

- Home
- About us
- Freelancer
    o Book publicist
- Speaker
    o Writer
    o Dare to Fly
    o Rough trade
    o The Knowing
    o Do it Yourself Websites
- Contact Us

That soon developed into this:

- Home
- About Paula
    o Freelancer
        - *Clients*
    o Book publicist
    o Speaker
    o Writer
        - *Dare to Fly*
        - *Rough trade*
        - *The Knowing*
- Workshops
    o SEO Masterclass
    o PR Masterclass
    o Do it Yourself Website Masterclass
    o Win a workshop
- Book
    o Do it Yourself Websites
    o Who should read the book
    o Win a signed book
- Social Links
- Contact Us
    o Mailing List

By now it will have probably changed yet again and you may see something completely different to this list. The important point is that your navigation map will be changing constantly as your website grows and develops. So, start with the basics and when you get the hang of it go back and take another view on how visitors should navigate through your site.

Have a look at my other sites to see far more complex navigation in action: www.remoteemployment.com and www.remoteworkerawards.com. Also take a look at our experts' websites and see how their navigation works. And don't forget to check your competitors' navigation as well as your favourite sites.

Summary
Today we started to understand the terms used in creating a website menu. We also explored various options for your new site's navigation map and learnt how to keep all the family in the right place.

Checklist
❑ Domain Name
❑ Home Page
❑ About Us
❑ Search

❑ Parents
❑ Children
❑ Terms and Conditions
❑ Contact Us

Day 4: Free Websites

The Buzz

After the intensive tasks of the last few days, we are getting closer to visualising the final result. Are you getting excited?

While writing this book, all the warm memories of building our brand and navigation came flooding back, as well as the scary, risky ones. Today, we will go one step further and determine exactly what kind of site you will venture into.

There are a number of different options open to you, from a simple blog, to a freebie el' cheapo thingy-majig or a fancy-dancy specially built site. Whatever your preference, we're all set to get cracking on what kind of site to choose.

Free V Paid

We are going to cover a variety of different ways for you to get your own website up and running pretty quickly.

A bespoke site is one that is completely tailored to your needs. Bespoke sites can be expensive and time consuming to build and costs can run into hundreds of thousands. But, before you fall off your chair, they don't all fit into that category. Depending on what you need, some may only cost a few thousand. There are developers who offer great sites which are bespoke in design, layout and functionality.

Others offer 'off the shelf' sites that they have already developed before and then they offer you the software at a reduced cost with only brand changes to be made. These are referred to as instant sites. An instant site is one that often comes as an extra when you buy a domain name. Alternatively you can buy a domain name when you sign up for a pay monthly site. This way you can pay it off and eventually own the site outright.

There are also similar optionswhere you effectively rent the website - these are known as online hosted solutions.

Basically, both of these hosted solutions give you templates to choose from with easy layout options and away you go. We will be going into this in more depth in the next few chapters so let's first cover the cheaper, quicker and easier options.

I would recommend testing all the free sites listed below to see which you find the easiest to use and, when you're getting along like next best friends, then decide which one is for keeps. Or move on to Hosted Websites to see if there is a better option for your online adventure.

Blog Website

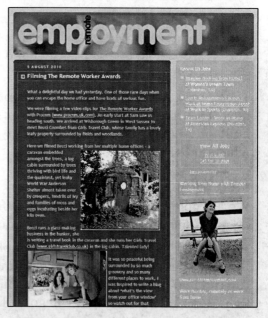

A Blog is a great way of getting online in a flash. A blog is an abbreviated version of 'weblog', which is a term used to describe web sites that chronicle or log information. However, they can be, and often are, used as a website.

If you are going to set up a blog alongside your site, try and retain your brand. This example shows the Remote Employment brand reflected in a standard Blogger template. More about this in a tick.

SO, WHAT IS A BLOG?

Where've you been? Living under a rock? That's what I was told a couple of years ago and had to get up to speed pronto on blogs and blogging. Let me tell you, blogging is not everyone's 'cuppa tea'.

First off, you have to be dedicated to be a full time blogger, and if you are passionate about a subject and have lots to say and share, this could be a good option for you.

A Blog is clever software that allows you to post articles and enables easy interaction with your audience; people can comment on your topic and you can reply. Blogs feature a wide range of diary-type entries from personal to corporate across a huge assortment of subjects. Some are personal journals of the author's daily life, while others are meanderings on topics or ramblings on current or newsworthy issues.

Most companies have a blog alongside, or integrated into, their website. However, because a blog is a type of website, you can also run your website through blogging software.

SOME THINGS THAT BLOGS HAVE IN COMMON:

- Content listed in chronological order, with the newest on top
- Archives of older articles
- Functionality that enables people to leave comments
- A blogroll, which is a list of other related sites
- Feeds such as RSS or other files – which helps other sites pick up and share your content with links back
- A wide variety of templates or 'themes'
- Side columns with all sorts of widgets and gadgets

If you are starting out and not sure what you want to do, try setting up a free blog in Blogger or Word Press. This will give you start up experience on working with a blog website. It will also show you how to add pages and content, and how to implement widgets and gadgets into your site. Go to blogger.com and/or wordpress.com for a quick snoop around. Depending on your product or service, you can run an online business through a blog for free

 Widget: a cool gadget that can be set up in various online platforms to create nifty tools.

Brand Your Blog

When setting up your blog implement your new brand or ensure your maintain an existing corporate image. I know this isn't easy when you have to stick to the templates library, but you can still choose colours, fonts and themes to closely match your main website.

You can also insert your logo into a header to reinforce your brand. If you're going to use a Blog to start up a website, choose a template that reflects your brand as discussed in yesterday's chapter so when you're ready to start a website, it all ties in just grand!

Click on Remote Employment's blog to see what we did to get as close to our brand as possible: remoteemployment.blogspot.com.

Ensure your Blogger account reflects your website name or keywords in the title. In one of my workshops, a lady wanted something really 'buzzy' and brainstormed all sorts of names, but in the end the best advice is to go with your company name spiced with keywords. Go back to your notes on naming your site and remind yourself of the important points we discussed.

Blogs should be updated often and generally provide a personal view or insight to a business. It can be a struggle to maintain a regular blogging personality. As in most small or micro businesses, there is so much to juggle before even thinking about blogging regularly. An idea that works well is to schedule blog posts so that your articles are published automatically on a certain date. This is handy if you write a batch blogs when you have some time as they can be published individually over a period of time.

There are also Blogs that charge a monthly fee, such as Type Pad. They do give you the option to have a free trial with Basic, Plus, Pro and Business Class options: www.typepad.com.

WordPress Blogs

Wordpress.com offers a free service, which gets you started in minutes. You can choose various templates and, just by clicking on them, you will get a preview to see how your blog will look.

In this screenshot, can you see the word 'Edit' under 'Contact'? That's because I am signed into my dashboard (the control panel) and all I have to do is click the edit button to change that page.

When you are choosing a template look at all the elements such as tabs, right hand and left hand design. In my blog, I liked the idea of having the tabs across the top, which made it feel more like a website because you could add various pages. Choose a template to suit your needs. By the way, mine is called 'Misty Look' by Sadish.

POSTS MENU

You only need to click on the links for adding or editing posts (your web blog message or content).

When you add a post, you will be able to include images and links to another blog or your main website.

LINKS MENU

Not dissimilar to 'bogroll', a Blogroll is a long strand of all your favourite web links. Simply click 'add new' or 'edit' to make changes.

PAGES

By clicking on the 'Pages' link, a new window opens which allows you to add new pages and edit your existing pages.

When you add a new page the right hand column gives you the option to choose a Parent page (we covered this yesterday) and the ability to rank or order your new page by priority in your navigation.

If you're using a blog as your main site to start off then get out your notes and navigation map and add pages according to your plan. You can also change this at any time.

WIDGETS

Wordpress also offers widgets in your dashboard that can easily be moved around by dragging and dropping. In the widgets window you will see all manner of gadgets you can use in your side bars, from a calendar, RSS, search, blogroll, recent posts, tag cloud and twitter.

Drag and drop, then preview. If you don't like the look on the live site, simply go back and change it. Easy as that!

TO TAG OR NOT TO TAG

Adding tags to your blog will help to optimise your blog or website in search engines. Tags are ideally single words or phrases listed alphabetically and act as your keyword(s). Other bloggers or browsers may find your blog due to your use of these tags.

Wordpress tags your pages, which in turn helps you get found by search engines. A Tag Cloud is meant to help readers quickly identify what type of post you have written and what type of posts you have covered.

If you have a website and want more control, you can download software from Wordpress.org. This is separate from the dot com site and is completely customisable, and can be used within your own hosted site rather than at another web location. More on this in the next chapter.

Free Websites

Just as you can get online in minutes with a blog, there are similar free sites. They all have different benefits and features so take a good look at the ones I have listed below. See if you can find some of your own. Research each of them in turn. Take the tests and trials before you spend too much and effort developing your site on one platform as another solution might be better suited to your requirements and website brief.

Here is a list of some sites I found:

- Amazon Advantage
- Amazon aStore
- Drupal
- GBBO
- Moonfruit
- Joomla
- Wordpress (.org)

Pros:
- ✓ Easy to install or get online
- ✓ Logical admin interface
- ✓ Some are suited to corporate websites
- ✓ Others offer quick website options
- ✓ Many extensions available
- ✓ Core platform is stable, reliable and well maintained
- ✓ Most have simple learning curve

Cons:
- ✗ Some extensions are chargeable
- ✗ Hard to scale up to a large website without spending money on developers
- ✗ Some platforms, such as Joomla have an elitist community making it hard for beginners to learn it's inner workings
- ✗ Might not be entirely search engine friendly if out of the box

- ✘ Hard to integrate other scripts and packages into your site
- ✘ Some security concerns with 3rd party extensions
- ✘ May have steep learning curve

aStore

Amazon is one of the most trusted online stores so you can't go wrong here. If you don't have products to sell, but would like to feature related products on your website, try using Amazon's aStore programme. aStore by Amazon is an Associates product that gives you the power to create a professional online store that can be embedded within, or linked to your website in minutes and without any programming skills.

FEATURE AMAZON PRODUCTS
- Create a dedicated shopping area on your website in minutes
- Keep visitors on your site longer as they shop
- Select the Amazon products to feature
- Include all Amazon products or choose categories
- Earn commission from sales, although this is largely dependent on a high traffic rate

HOW DOES IT WORK?
Easy! With four simple configuration pages, you can create and customise your aStore in minutes. No programming is necessary as the aStore wizard will guide you through the process and generate a URL which you can link to or embed into your site.

OFFER A SHOPPING CART
- Gain the trust of your customers with a professional online store, without ever writing any code
- Offer a shopping cart for multiple item purchases
- Check Amazon.co.uk

HOW TO GET STARTED
1. If you are not a member of the Associates programme, start by joining here: http://associates.amazon.co.uk/join
2. If you are already a member of the Associates programme, visit the aStore section of Associates Central
3. Check out more details: http://astore.amazon.co.uk

STEP BY STEP
1. Customise the look and feel of your store by selecting a colour theme, specifying the store title and including a link to your logo.
2. You can include your logo in the header.
3. Select each page type and add widgets to provide your visitors with useful content and an opportunity to up-sell.

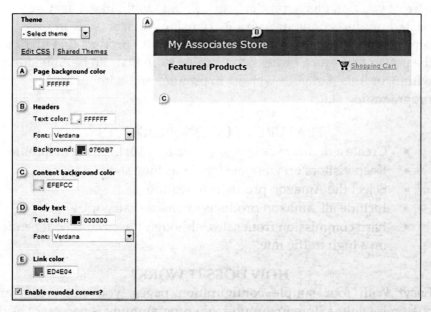

Here you have three options:

1. Link to your aStore as a stand-alone site
Make your aStore a stand-alone section of your website by adding a 'Store' link to your main site navigation bar that links directly to your new store. This is the easiest way to integrate your aStore. However, it will appear to your users as if they are leaving your website when visiting your it.

2. Embed your aStore using an inline frame
An inline frame is a great way to embed your aStore into any existing or new page on your website. This method of embedding your aStore will appear to your visitors as if the aStore is part of your website and enable them to shop without leaving your site.

3. Embed your aStore using a frameset

Frame your aStore into your Web site using a Frameset by placing your aStore in one frame and your Web site's navigation in another frame. Embedding your store will appear to your visitors as if the store is part of your website and enable them to shop without leaving. However, to do this you will probably need some assistance from a developer so check it out first.

Here's an aStore I created using a stand-alone site.

After you have decided how you want to embed your aStore, go to the aStore link in your account to add products.

ADD A CATEGORY PAGE

Or you can select from Amazon's categories list, which is a dynamic way to keep up to date with latest items, bestsellers etc. It goes without saying that it's best to create store pages that are relevant to the content of your Web site.

This part can be a bit confusing - you have to click on the edit button on your aStore link – the image below shows where the edit button is located so you can add items to your aStore.

Click the "Edit" button to add items to your aStore

STEP BY STEP

For each page, you have three options for selecting products from Amazon.com's inventory:

1. Hand pick products for each of your aStore pages.

2. Display products from Amazon Listmania lists.

3. Display products that belong to selected Amazon categories or sub-categories. These pages will automatically show best selling products for the selected categories.

4. Due to the extensive inventory available on Amazon.com, you can streamline the content of a category page to include products that contain specific keywords. This is ideal if you only want to feature items for certain topics within your site.

FOR EXAMPLE: you might only want to show beauty books, so you would select books and show the keywords you want to feature.

WIDGETS

Amazon gives you gorgeous tools to show off their products on your site with search boxes and advertising widgets.

Search Box

Customise your store's look and feel with nifty tools and gadgets. Here's one I made earlier; literally minutes after joining I created this search box. As the image shows, all you do is choose which type of search box you want and Amazon gives you the code, which you then copy and paste into your page.

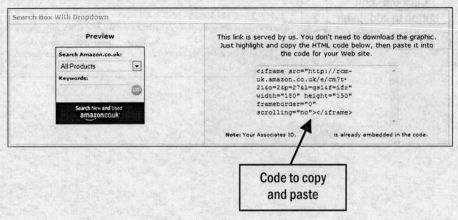

Carousel

I had great fun creating a Carousel Banner, which can be added to your Blogger site as well as a raft of other websites and blogs. You can also copy and paste the HTML code that Amazon provides straight into a web page. For this Carousel banner, I used 'Book Bestsellers'.

Ferris Wheel

Choose this option for adding a tower or skyscraper banner to your site. I used 'Hot Book New Releases' for a Ferris Banner. See more on how to implement advertising and banners during the next few days and then hop back over to this section to insert banners into your site.

> **FOR EXAMPLE:** if you are a new writer why not set up a book club to encourage readers interested in a particular type of book. Let's say travel books. You can set up banners with different travel topical books on your site. If you are serious about getting yourself published, this will help to build a 'platform' of followers.

NO CHARGES

All Associates have access to an aStore, and there are no fees associated with building a store for your site. Lastly, if you do go for this aStore, please feel free to feature my book. Find it on Amazon under the title or by following this link and show it off to others – it could help more people get online:

www.amazon.com/dp/1907498354/ref=nosim?tag=createasuccessfulwebsite-21

Amazon Advantage

The Advantage Programme is a simple, direct and profitable way to sell your items through the world's leading online retailer.

Amazon Advantage is a way for authors, publishers, labels, and studios of all sizes to promote and sell their items on Amazon.

WHY JOIN AMAZON ADVANTAGE?

The Amazon name is immediately recognised, making it easy for millions of customers worldwide to find, discover and buy your items.

TOP REASONS TO SELL ON AMAZON

- Open 24/7
- Customers view and purchase your products on Amazon
- Amazon is a leading web site and a trusted brand
- Millions of online shoppers every day
- Makes buying your products a snap
- Helps your customers make quick, easy, worry-free purchases
- Amazon notifies you by email when an order has been placed
- You simply pack and ship your item to the customer
- Or you can sign up for 'Fulfilment by Amazon' and let Amazon do the shipping for you
- Amazon deposits payment into your bank account every 14 days and sends an email notifying you that your payment has been sent

How easy is that? Makes me wish I had products to sell!

LINK

Have a good look around Amazon before you commit:
http://advantage.amazon.co.uk/gp/vendor/public/professional

Drupal

Drupal is a free software package that allows an individual or a community of users to easily publish, manage and organise a wide variety of content on a website. Drupal is an Open Source project, which means there are hundreds of people, and most of them experienced developers, all over the world working on the software and so you get the benefit of their experience and expertise for free.

It offers a broad range of features and services including user administration, publishing workflow, discussion boards, news aggregation, metadata for optimisation and XML publishing for content sharing purposes.

Tens of thousands of people and organisations have used Drupal to power scores of different web sites. For example, Pimp My Site Club and Babyworld are powered by Drupal.

TYPES OF DRUPAL SITES

- Intranet sites
- Personal websites or blogs
- Community portals
- Discussion boards
- Corporate websites

- E-commerce shops
- Resource directories
- Social Networking sites
- Personal websites or blogs

Drupal is perhaps the most complex CMS availabile, but it is without question the most powerful and flexible. The downside is that it has quite a steep learning curve because it uses a fundamentally different approach to website architecture.

It is perfectly suited to community and membership sites, with many social features built in. It has an API, meaning it can play ball with other applications and websites, such as Twitter and Facebook. It has a massive community of dedicated friendly developers, who create and maintain literally thousands of extensions, which will cover just about any requirement you could ever dream up.

Drupal has been successfully used on the following high profile sites:

- www.whitehouse.gov
- www.london.gov.uk
- www.data.gov.uk
- www.economist.com

- www.nasa.org
- www.bbcmagazines.com
- www.mtv.co.uk
- www.greenpeace.org

Using Drupal may be overkill if you only need a small brochure site, but knowing what you can achieve highlights just how dynamic it is. Remember your 'Think Big' future plans. Start small and grow with Drupal.

Pros:

- ✓ Robust and secure platform
- ✓ No up-scaling problems - you can go from a small site to large traffic magnet, without issues
- ✓ Flexibility - it can do just about anything you can imagine
- ✓ Friendly free support and development network
- ✓ Powerful user permission system
- ✓ Different roles and permission for users
- ✓ One module to install for a fully functioning e-commerce shop
- ✓ Integration with other sites and applications

Cons:

- ✗ Tougher learning curve than alternatives
- ✗ Used primarily for large community sites with 10,000 plus visitors per day
- ✗ Not designed for out of the box business websites
- ✗ It's made by programmers, not designers - it will do what you want, but may not look pretty so you may need some bespoke work done by a developer

DRUPAL SUMMARY

Drupal is not easy to get to grips with, although the new version 7.0 has several changes in usability which new users will applaud. Drupal stands head and shoulders above other CMS platforms in terms of flexibility and power.

Once you grasp the basics, you have the tools at your disposal to make your business website blast spots off the competition. All that's required is your time and imagination.

LINK

www.drupal.org

You can view tutorials on Drupal here:
http://php.opensourcecms.com/free/videos.php#drupal

CLARE MEDDEN ON DRUPAL...

Let's be honest, in the next ten years we're going to see huge jumps in access to the internet and how it gets used in people's everyday lives. If you want to use the internet to enhance your business properly, and take advantage of these developments, Drupal is the way to go. If you don't have time, or the inclination to learn the system, why not consider hiring a developer to set it up for you. You'll end up with a future-proof, stable, secure website that can expand and grow not only with your business, but also with the pace of technology.

GBBO

Businesses of every type and size need to be found online. Use GBBO's simple online tool to create your first website with no technical knowledge needed. And you can update your site from any computer in the world, for free.

WHO ARE GBBO?

Getting British Business Online is a joint initiative between Google, BT, Enterprise UK and e-skills UK to get 100,000 UK businesses online. They've joined the campaign to help local businesses make the most of the Internet's huge potential.

They aim to target 1.5 million UK businesses that do not currently have a website, giving them the opportunity to create a free professional website along with access to training and support.

Businesses that sign up to Getting British Business Online will be given a free .co.uk web address that will be automatically registered in Google's search engine, a new 'wizard' tool that will help you create a website in 20 minutes and ways to attract new customers online.

BT will offer free phone support to participants, PayPal will soon enable businesses with a GBBO-powered website to turn your site into an e-commerce platform in just a few clicks. This means you can begin selling to customers and accepting payments quickly and securely via the web.

THREE SIMPLE STEPS

1. Choose a website address.
2. Select and customise a template.
3. Publish your website.

HOW IT WORKS

To get your free professional business website, all you need to do is provide a few basic details about your business, such as your address and a quick description of what you do. Then the easy-to-use 'website wizard' does the rest. You don't need any computer skills, it shouldn't take more than 20 minutes, and it won't cost you a penny.

WHAT YOU GET

- A free .co.uk address
- Free updating and customisation
- Access to new customers
- Website visitor monitoring
- Website-enhancing gadgets

TOP REASONS TO USE GBBO

Grow your business:

- Attract new customers with a free listing on Google Maps
- Allow potential customers to find you and place orders for your products
- Make it easy for your customers to buy online with PayPal
- Comes gift wrapped with a 'Free Marketing Toolkit' that includes:
  - o A Promotional Email template
  - o Press release
  - o Website newsletter
  - o 'How-to' guide

WHY IS THIS ALL FREE?

Because GBBO is working with Google and BT they're able to offer you a free website for 2 years. After that you'll only have to pay a few pounds to renew your domain name for a further 2 years. You're not tied in to a contract and they won't put ads on your site without your permission.

LINK

www.gbbo.co.uk

Google Base

Another good place that could help in your quest to get online is Google Base. Technically, it is not actually a website package, but as you don't pay to list your items on Google Base, it gives anyone with products to sell the ability to get online quickly.

QUICK FACTS

Google Base is a place where you can easily submit all types of online and offline content, which they make searchable on Google. If your content isn't online yet then they'll host it for you.

- Promote your products for free
- Items you submit to Google Base might be found through other Google tools like Google's search engine and Google Maps.
- You can submit information about all types of online and offline content to Google Base via a data feed or Google Base API. They do reserve the right to review all items in order to ensure they comply with the Google Base T&Cs.
- Google Base enables you to add attributes describing your content, so that searchers can easily find it.

CHARGES

You can create and display any number of items using Google Base for free.

LINK

www.base.google.com

Joomla

Joomla is an award-winning content management system (CMS), which enables you to build websites and powerful online applications. Many aspects, including its ease-of-use and extensibility, have made Joomla one of the most popular choices for website software. Best of all, Joomla is another open source solution that is freely available to everyone.

Clare vouches for Joomla as it is a solid, well established CMS, with a wide following. It was a fork of another CMS platform called Mambo, which is still maintained and available today, but the resounding success of Joomla made it the best choice of platform between the two.

Joomla seems ideally suited to corporate websites. If the main part of your business is offline, but you need some kind of online presence, Joomla may be a good fit. It offers most of the features that a simple website would need and more add-ons are available, although many are not free.

JOOMLA SUMMARY

This is an ideal solution if you don't have time and money to spend on a website. Out of the box it should provide everything you want to get a professional looking business website up and running in days. It expands reasonably well up to a certain size, but if you need more features it can become more expensive to develop.

LINK

www.joomla.org

Moonfruit

Moonfruit is another great piece of kit that can get anyone up and running in a morning or afternoon.

If you want to change text, you simply click on it and change it. If you want to move an image, just haul it across the page, or drag the corners to change its size.

There is no technology to learn, no techie code, no form filling, just quick and easy tools that work wonders for seeing your site in action right under your fingertips. There is a little box called 'View My Site' and each time you make a change you can click this to see the changes on the live site.

IT OFFERS

- Free domain name
- 5 email mailboxes
- Multiple sites per account
- Increased storage and bandwidth
- E-commerce tools via PayPal
- Google Adwords vouchers up to £50
- Free site up to 15 pages

Moonfruit is available as both a free and a paid-for service with the free version of Moonfruit having some restricted features. Subscription based Moonfruit packs are available at different prices. None of the templates on offer will show ads or carry Moonfruit branding, so the site is completely yours! I created a Moonfruit website on a Saturday afternoon.

The Moonfruit editing tools are built using Adobe Flash because it allows them to offer a genuine 'drag and drop' WYSIWYG (What you see is what you get) interface that makes Moonfruit so easy to use.

Although Flash is often criticised for not being search engine friendly, Moonfruit extracts the content from your site and publishes it in HTML too so it is available to the widest range of browsers and is correctly indexed and listed by search engines.. This gives you all the benefits of a slick easy to use Flash interface without any downside.

INTRO TO MOONFRUIT

A quick intro to Moonfruit shows you that its drag and drop editor is extremely easy to use. Although Moonfruit has a website editor, it is more like a graphic design tool because it gives you control over the design details of your site.

SOCIAL MEDIA

Social media integration is important in a professional site nowadays and Moonfruit allows you to create 'members only' pages and give edit rights to different users of your site. Moonfruit also features a snippet widget which gives you access to a variety of 3rd party tools such as Facebook and Twitter. This all links in with your social networks so that you can send messages out from your site to Facebook or Twitter, and invite people to become members of your site from other networks.

ADDING A TWITTER FEED

1. Click insert (+ button), which opens basic objects box.
2. Click insert 'HTML nippet.'
3. This drops in a snippet box.
4. Click in the snippet, which opens a snippet editor.
5. Hit 'Get Snippet'
6. You will be logged into your Twitter account to customise your snippet.
7. Choose your settings, preferences, appearance and dimensions, which shows you how the feed will appear on your site.
8. You can test the settings and then finish and grab the code.
9. The code appears in your snippet box on your site and you click 'Apply'.
10. View your site to see the Twitter feed. You can also move this snippet box anywhere on your page. How cool is that?

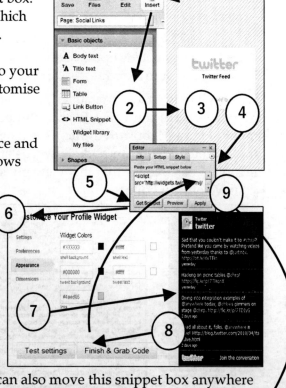

The free edition of Moonfruit has a free library of images, animations and widgets for you to use in your site. They are available in a range of styles, which can be customised to help you achieve the look and content you want.

SEARCH ENGINE OPTIMISATION (SEO)

As SEO (search engine optimisation) is so vital, Moonfruit have taken the initiative to ensure their sites are optimised for search engines by default.

It's easy-peasy to add metadata. Once you have built and edited your Moonfruit site, you can add tracking code from Google Analytics to monitor your Moonfruit traffic. This diagram shows that when you are in page mode, you can add keywords and a page description into the metadata box. Notice that the 'view my site' button is always visible in your Moonfruit editor.

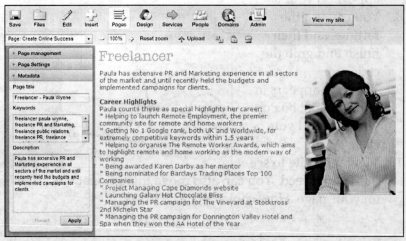

For a comprehensive explanation and in-depth detail on how to use keywords and 'On Page Optimisation', please read my book *Pimp My Site*!

Other tools, such as Google AdSense, give you the chance to earn an income from your site as well.

Within a week of uploading my paulawynne.moonfruit.com site, it was right up high on the first page of Google!

Okay, I know that the site is sprinkled with references to my name and therefore much easier for any search engine to find. And, I know that my name is not highly competitive but it performed well for me before I moved my site to a pay monthly platform and hopefully it will do the same for your free site.

An unlimited number of additional features can be added to your site from Google Gadgets, Amazon widgets to games, e-commerce tools, RSS feeds, video and music players and much, much more. All you do is drag one of these widgets onto your page, click 'Get Snippet' and the software does the rest.

Once you have approved the link, it even gives you the HTML to add into your snippet box. The flexible image tool gives you the option of scaling, rotating and making images transparent.

In addition you can include galleries, slideshows, and animations to create a unique look on your site. This is great for photographers, but there is a limit to the amount of images you can have on a free site.

And if that isn't enough, you can also sell things on your Moonfruit site. Start trading online with their PayPal widgets and 'buy now' buttons that link directly to a PayPal shopping cart.

Include clean and clear product pages and then add e-commerce functions using their HTML widget like PayPal's Storefront, or Amazon's affiliate widgets. There's nothing holding you back, so start selling your products now!

You can either use a Moonfruit domain, such as paulawynne. moonfruit.com or you can add your own domain when you are happy with your newly designed site.

MOONFRUIT FAVICON

You'll remember that a Favicon is short for favourite icon and is that tiny logo seen on branded sites beside the URL domain name. If you bookmark a site, it displays the Favicon in your 'Favourites' folder.

I gave you a few sites to try and showed you how to insert your own. Go to your Moonfruit CMS admin section editor > Design > Page Master > Insert Border or Icon. And hey presto, you have a cute little Favicon of your very own!

LINK

www.moonfruit.com

Squidoo

Squidoo, www.squidoo.com, also offer free websites or, as they call them, Lenses. You can create as many as you want within one account. I've set one up quickly to show you what can be done, but, as I didn't have much time it is a little bare and doesn't have all the mod-cons of my actual site. You can see my Squidoo Lens at www.squidoo.com/paulawynne to get an idea. However, do have a good look at the large variety of sites on their home page as some 'squids' have really gone to town.

Squidoo makes it easy for you to find useful overview pages. They believe it's also a fun and simple way to publish your own lenses for free and share what you care about.

Their motto is: Get found, get followed, get influential. Squidoo is also classed as a social media tool, but I have chosen to add it to this section on free websites because you could use it as your main website and it's free.

Squidoo reckon that you can make a lens for just about anything, a CV or resume, a birthday wish list, a collection of your favourite books, a signpost page for Google or whatever you can think of.

THE SQUIDOO HOMEPAGE

For those who like to start at the beginning, browse some of the top lenses to see what they look like (and maybe get some ideas for your own lenses).

THE LENS OF THE DAY

Discover a great looking lens. They pick one lens, every day, and spotlight it to the community. It's a great award to receive if you get picked, and a fun way to learn about other lenses. See their lens of the day page here and then give it a whirl: http://blogs.squidoo.com/lensoftheday

THE OFFICIAL SQUIDBLOG

They post updates at http://blogs.squidoo.com/squidblog/ whenever there's a big update, or new features to know about. You don't really have to subscribe to this in order to get Squidoo, but if you plan to roll up your sleeves and really work on your lenses, it could help.

THE SQUIDOO COMMUNITY

Meet other lens masters, find tips and tricks for getting started and making your lenses rock. Their motto: Never fear! The Squids are here. Fellow lens masters, just like you, are eager to help if asked sweetly.

THE SQUIDOO RECIPE

Download this E-book written by Seth Godin and Megan Casey. It's a few dozen pages long and will fire you up to stun fellow Squids: http://sethgodin.typepad.com/changethis/files/TheJoyofSquidoo.pdf

START A NEW LENS

You'll find lots of links and buttons around the site that you can use to start a new lens, so here's just one more shortcut if you're ready to get going right now: http://www.squidoo.com/wizard/step1

EARNING MONEY

See this link for top tips on earning payments from your lens: www.squidoo.com/paymentfaq

LINK

Squidoo: www.squidoo.com

Weebly

I found Weebly easy to use and had some fun dragging and dropping and trying out every tool and gadget I could lay my paws on.

Setting up an account is quick and you can use your own domain or one of theirs, such as paulawynne.weebly.com

Once you're in, you'll see their handy drag and drop editor where you can set up your pages, choose your design, add elements and include other advanced settings.

The setting tab gives you the chance to verify your site and add tracking code for Google. The following screenshot shows how to edit site settings and add Meta keywords in Weebly.

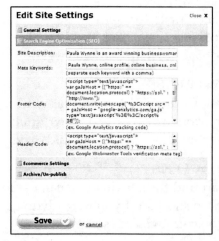
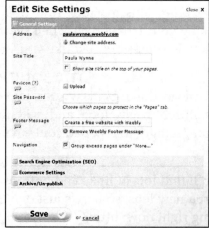

Under the tab called 'elements' you can drag and drop a paragraph, a paragraph with an image and contact form into your empty page. In the 'pages' tab you can move the order of your pages around by simply dragging and dropping them.

The 'multimedia' tab gives you everything from adding files, photo galleries, video, flash, Google maps, flickr photo slideshows and YouTube videos. The 'more' tab gives you RSS feeds, custom HTML, forums, online bookings, online polls and even a page divider. All so easy to use, it really is child's play. The 'revenue' tab offers Google Adsense.

What's Google Adsense? It's a flexible easy way to earn revenue online. You get paid for displaying Google Adsense adverts on your site, where you can customise and target the ads to match your site's look and feel and then track the results with reports. All for free. More on this later in our Revenue chapter.

One word of warning, DON'T click on 'Fun'; Weebly has a huge selection of games and you'll be engrossed and playing like a kid with a new toy! Finally, you can opt to buy an upgraded account for a small fee, or purchase your own domain. There are countless other features that you'll have to discover for yourself.

LINK

www.weebly.com

Wordpress

WordPress started as just a blogging system, but has evolved to be used as a full content management system (CMS) through the thousands of plugins, widgets, and themes available.

Since then it has grown to be the largest self-hosted blogging tool in the world, used on millions of sites and seen by tens of millions of people every day. Wordpress is one of the most widely used platforms, hosting over 200 million websites, mainly because it's simple to use, flexible and easy to install.

WordPress is also an Open Source project. It enables you to use it for anything from your cat's home page to a Fortune 500 web site without paying anyone a license fee.

WORDPRESS.ORG V WORDPRESS.COM

WordPress.org is completely customisable and can be used for almost anything. As I mentioned early on in this book, there is a service called WordPress.com, which lets you get started with a new and free WordPress-based blog in seconds, but varies in several ways and is less flexible than the WordPress.org you download and install yourself.

WordPress.org is an ideal starting block and Clare says the installation process is painless. Within minutes you will have a working website that can be updated and maintained through an administration section.

However, because it was initially designed as a blogging system, adding commonly used website features, such as e-commerce, user permissions and workflow queues can be a little more complex.

Sadly, it is a victim of its own success in that it is targeted by spam bots and hackers. So don't allow un-moderated comments on your Wordpress site, and prepare to see more gambling adverts than you can shake a stick at.

Pros:
- ✓ Simple to use, suitable for a beginners
- ✓ Wide range of pre-made templates available
- ✓ No programming or server experience required
- ✓ Many popular add on modules available for free
- ✓ Perfectly suited to small simple sites, especially brochure-style sites, a CV profile or biog

✓ Friendly 'theming' system, with hundreds free to download

Cons:

✗ Often targeted by spammers and hackers

✗ Difficult to adapt to exact requirements without delving into the PHP code

✗ Blogging platform, that has been expanded on, causing some limitations

✗ 3rd party modules often cause unexpected results and conflict with each other

WORDPRESS SUMMARY

Great for blogs, small brochure sites, or anyone new to content management systems, but lacks the power and extendibility to run a complex site, without in-depth programming knowledge. Keep an eye out for spam.

LINK

www.wordpress.org

Car Story

Clare believes that if Drupal, Joomla and Wordpress were cars...

Wordpress would be a small 2 door hatchback. An ideal starter car to get you on the road and driving about. It may not have loads of space or the best technical features, and it rattles a bit in 3rd gear, but it's totally practical and efficient.

Joomla is your luxury saloon. Polished and shiny, with comfortable leather seats, making the passenger's ride smooth and trouble free. It won't win any races, and it doesn't stand out from all the other similar cars on the road, yet it has prestige and reliability. But beware; the optional extras can cost an arm and a leg!

Drupal is a classic car. It's the car you've always wanted to own, but never had the time to find. It's got a huge following of fans, who loyally patch up any rust, or repair any dents and share information with you. They build these mind-blowing, bolt-on modifications for your classic car for free!

There's one that turns it into a hovercraft. Another that turns it into a helicopter, a monster truck, a jet powered rocket ship. You can even build your own and share them with the other classic car drivers.

So, to own and maintain a classic car, you're going to have to roll up your sleeves from time to time and get your hands dirty or find yourself a reliable mechanic.

Summary

Today we ventured into the world of websites and realised there is no harm in choosing a simple blog to start off your new online business.

We delved into the abundance of great free sites out there and even if we want an imaginative project we can still get it for nearly nothing or even completely free.

Now, it's time to get stuck into paid sites. Even though most of us will flinch at the word 'paid', many paid sites don't have to have the 'ouch' factor and may be precisely what you're looking for.

Checklist

❑ Domain Name search
❑ Consider options for hosting
❑ Check out free trials on paid sites
❑ Amazon Advantage
❑ aStore

❑ Drupal
❑ GBBO
❑ Joomla
❑ Moonfruit
❑ Squidoo
❑ Weebly
❑ WordPress

Day 5: Hosted Websites

Variety Bucket

Just as you would host guests at a party or event, there are numerous website providers who will 'host' your site for you and throw in a bundle of entertainment, party poppers and hampers of goodies.

In this chapter we'll discuss various online hosted sites before moving on to sites that you can pay off on a monthly basis and eventually own.

Website Software

There are various software packages available for purchase, from the simplest to the most complicated, so be careful before hitting the buy button. Have a good look and compare the different packages to be certain it will suit your requirements. Once bought and tested, you can't simply return it because you can't use it.

Features

Make sure the solution you choose offers a large variety of templates. Study this list before making a purchase. I didn't have space to list all the ones I found so browse a list of sites to try before you choose.

Pros:

- ✓ Pretty much cheap and affordable
- ✓ Most are quick and easy to get online
- ✓ Lots of nifty gadgets, buttons and bows
- ✓ Huge time saver
- ✓ No HTML knowledge or coding needed
- ✓ Some integrate with other tools, such as Photoshop, Flash and eBay

Cons:

- ✗ Could be restricting because of template use
- ✗ Check if Windows or Mac compatible
- ✗ May be hard to use, thus steep learning curve
- ✗ Often no human support

How To Choose Website Software

Consider the following issues and features when shopping for web design software.

GO FOR SIMPLICITY

A few pages, a couple of images and a logo could be all you need to get up and running. Don't try and build a complex site before you've had a chance to play around with a blog site or an easy template site.

Decide how much techie stuff you want to learn. You may enjoy playing with various web development tools, but don't get sucked in and go overboard with things you don't need right now.

Also, don't spend time playing when you should be getting your site online and optimised; it is an easy trap to fall into with the variety available. It can be so much fun - I'm guilty of that sin!

SYSTEM REQUIREMENTS

Only choose software designed for your operating system. Although you may be a fuddy-duddy and still have one of those antique computers now only available in a PC museum, remember that slower computers perform better with simpler web design software.

USE WHAT YOU KNOW

Don't think you can design the ultimate site straight off. Start small and use what you know.

In one of my training workshops a lovely lady told me she was advised to use Dreamweaver, yet she hadn't even heard of a blog. Start small and move onto bigger plans when you're ready.

ESTABLISH YOUR NEEDS

After you have a look at the software available, think about your requirements. If you are selling a service that needs more face-to-face contact with clients you won't necessarily want full e-commerce software.

FEATURES

Refer to your navigation list and mark out the features your website needs. You should at least be able to add pages, images, logos, a search box, links and possibly some widgets and buttons. Ensure you get SEO tools with it or skip it and move on to the next one.

EXTRA BITS

Bonus features include a domain and hosting. Wizards are handy, but a drag and drop system is even better. Easy 'Publishing Assistants' will make life hassle free when you're ready to upload your site. And the facility to check your site in various browsers will ensure professionalism.

WEB 2.0

You know how fast web and mobile technology is moving, so if you get iPhone and SmartPhone templates thrown in, grab it. Even if you don't use them now, remember your future goals. Keep this in mind for when you're more adept at clever web techie stuff.

ROOM TO GROW

Give your site development room to manoeuvre. Even if you don't require certain tools now, keep your future growth in mind.

EASY EDITOR

There's nothing more painful than having an editor that won't allow you to perform basic functions, so if you want to make pretty pictures and constant changes, do pay attention to the editor. It will pay off in the long run to get one you're happy with.

PC OR WEB BASED

Some people prefer working offline and some software solutions offer this facility. However, do check out the web based offerings and compare the benefits. You can, of course, be 'virtual' if you use a hosted system. Being web based also provides the added advantage of monitoring stats through one login.

EBAY-ERS

If you currently run an eBay site, some providers offer the added bonus of eBay integration.

HUMAN

One final point, and a vitally important one too. Try to ensure that you can get access to a human being in the support team. Personally, I won't do business with any company that I can't speak to by phone. This is especially important for novices.

Microsoft FrontPage

Microsoft FrontPage is a simple Windows WYSIWYG editor with a familiar look, which makes you feel as if you are working in Microsoft Word. Along with a photo gallery, e-commerce, drawing tools and an easy to use editor, it comes with team management features.

Beginners might be attracted to FrontPage because it was designed to hide HTML code, thus making it straightforward for a learner to create a website. However, Microsoft has now replaced FrontPage with their Expression Studio Web Professional - a full graphic, video, and web design suite - which is available on a free trial.

Microsoft Expression Web

This professional Web tool comes with features that help you design, develop, and maintain a successful website. It has been designed for creative professionals. However, no technical background is required to start using Expression Web. Convenient task panes and menus help users build attractive and compelling web pages without knowing any markup or server code.

Experienced users will also appreciate the extensive features of Expression Web, such as the WYSIWYG editor, CSS, page preview, link checker, database connectivity, form wizard, XML and RSS editor, spell check, free templates and an FTP site manager to upload your website.

When you use Expression Web to create and manage your website, you have a variety of tools at your disposal. For example, validation alerts you to errors that could break links and page structure.

LINK
www.microsoft.com/expression

Dreamweaver

If you've used design software or Photoshop® before, you will find Dreamweaver® is the ultimate tool. Download a free trial of Dreamweaver® to see just how versatile it is. Design, develop, and maintain standards-based websites and applications all in one place.

In a nutshell, Adobe® Dreamweaver® CS5 software enables you to develop with PHP-based content management systems such as

WordPress, Joomla or Drupal and design with powerful CSS inspection tools.

This industry-leading web authoring tool empowers designers and developers to build websites with confidence. You can design visually or directly in code, develop pages with content management systems, and accurately test browser compatibility.

You may want to investigate doing a course to teach yourself how to use Dreamweaver®, either a one day seminar or master class or even long term learning through an organisation such as Home Learning College (HLC). I still aim to teach myself Dreamweaver® one day soon!

Find out more about studying at home for a web design course: www.remoteemployment.com/Study-At-Home.aspx

LINK
www.adobe.com/products/dreamweaver

Free Trial

Some paid sites provide easy to use software or a hosted solution and a free trial. If you are going to go for a paid site, *always* set up a free trial through their demo software before committing to any long term payments that may be a waste if you cannot use the software.

Take advantage of any web design software that offers free trials, such as designersi.com and coffeecup.com.

Coffee Cup

You can choose a new layout from a one to three column page theme or from their layout menu, which gives you a limited amount of templates to browse through. The downside here is that they charge for a wider range of templates. The quick start menu gives you the choice of how to build your page starting with a background image and colour schemes.

I feel that Coffee Cup is best suited to someone who has prior knowledge of HTML and website building, but click on the 'Free Trial' link at the bottom of the page and see for yourself.

LINK
www.coffeecup.com/software (also try the free stuff tab)

Designersi

Designersi.com (pronounced designers-eye) also claims to be an advanced website builder for small businesses. They state that they've made it easy and affordable for non-technical people to build, manage and market their website. You have access to *all* of the great features designersi.com has to offer, including E-commerce, eBay integration, editing and marketing tools.

LINK

www.designersi.com

Hosted Online Shops

There are a number of ways to get an online store and today we will cover all of them. Some are free to set up and then charge per transaction or sale.

Pros:

✓ Fairly cheap and affordable
✓ Choice of templates
✓ Quick and easy to get online
✓ Lots of nifty gadgets and buttons
✓ Saves time and hassle
✓ No HTML knowledge or coding needed

Cons:

✗ Check the rates they charge per sale
✗ Some may use Amazon, so you pay twice
✗ May be restrictive because of template use
✗ Check if there is phone support
✗ Extra features may require more cash outlay

Here is a list of some affordable hosted shop systems I found:

• BT Web Hosting
• Cartfly
• CafePress
• Etsy
• Ning
• Yahoo

If none of these ticks your box, search Google for terms such as 'free online shop', 'free hosted shop', 'free online store', 'hosted online store' and anything else that may be suitable to your industry sector. Or wait until later today when we discus 'Instant Pay Monthly Websites'.

BT Web Hosting

BT Web Hosting offers you a quick and easy way to create a website. It also provides a full suite of services to help small businesses get online, ranging from domain names, through to hosting and fully designed sites.

TOP REASONS TO USE BT

- Trusted provider
- Includes domain names
- Easy to build your own website
- UK based technical support
- Free 15 minute consultation on how to build a great site
- They can build the site for you - ask for quotes

BOTH PACKAGES INCLUDE

- Appointment scheduler allows customers to schedule appointments from your site
- Easy blog builder
- Live chat to integrate chat features into your website
- Easy site wizard
- Plug-in scripts to enhance your site
- Hit counter
- Guest book
- Easy site wizard
- Photo album
- Webmaster tools
- Log manager to manage your website log files
- Web stats
- File manager

PROFESSIONAL PACKAGE INCLUDES

- Ad manager to configure a banner ad server for your site

- Send email marketing messages to subscribed customers with 500 emails per month
- Easy site optimiser
- Advanced template manager - choose professional templates
- Website security - protect areas of your website with passwords
- Restore web site files from backup
- Site promoter - promote your website by submitting to the big search engines using this easy tool

CHARGES

You can get a .co.uk domain name from just £2.95 per year, which comes with email and web space as standard, all part of the hosting package.

Starter Pack

£5.00 per month

- Ideal for creating your first website
- 1 domain name included
- 5GB web space
- Easy site builder tool
- Over 300 templates
- 24/7 dedicated support

Professional Package

£15.00 per month

- Ideal for creating a feature rich website
- 2 domain names included
- Unlimited web space
- Over 1,000 customisable templates
- Search optimisation tool
- eMarketing capability
- 24/7 dedicated support

LINK

http://business.bt.com/domains-and-web-hosting/web-hosting/web-hosting-packages

Cartfly

Easily create a storefront and portable Mini-Shop to market and share across major social networks, blogs and websites.

WHAT IS CARTFLY

Cartfly is a quick and easy way to sell your products online, with no setup, annual or listing fees. This simple e-commerce tool allows anyone with a valid Amazon account, email address and a product to start selling!

You can customise the look of your new store and start selling items across the web. Cartfly gives you the code to embed your store into your favourite social networks, blogs and a personal web site.

You can even get friends and supporters to embed your store in *their* social network to boost visibility. Every sale made at *any* location comes directly back to you.

CHARGES

Cartfly make money when *you* make money, by charging a 3% transaction fee when you sell something. Please note that you may pay twice if they use Amazon to process payments, so check this out.

TOP REASONS TO USE CARTFLY

- Creating a store is free
- No setup or annual fees
- Instant Amazon payment processing
- Easy-to-use interface
- Customise your store
- Embed your store anywhere and everywhere
- Get your own free web address

HOW TO GET GOING

Getting started with Cartfly is easy. Before your fingers hit the keyboard, have these details handy:

- The basic information about your store
- A logo, photo, or some other image to show off your brand
- An email address for a valid Amazon account
- Product pictures, descriptions and prices

117

Here's what you do:

1. Click one of the 'Start Selling' buttons on Cartfly.com
2. Fill in the required information, using the 'Next' and 'Back' buttons to navigate through the setup process.
3. Once the initial setup process is complete, you are taken to your store's Admin section on Cartfly.com. You will see a blank area where your products will eventually be displayed.
4. Click 'Add Product'
5. Enter the product's name, price, tags, and description. Separate multiple product tags with commas, and think of them as categories that your products will be sorted by, not keywords that describe the product itself.
6. Click 'Next: Product Image'
7. Click 'Upload Product Image'
8. Browse your files to locate the image of the product. Select the file and click 'Open'
9. Once you see the image displayed, click 'Next: Product Options'
10. If you do not need to configure options for your product (size, colour, style, etc), then you can click 'Save and Close'
11. Otherwise, continue with adding options.
12. Click 'Add Option'
13. Enter the option name (size, colour, style etc.)
14. Enter the option values, separated by commas ('small, medium, large', 'red, green, blue', etc.)
15. When you have added all of your product's options, click 'Save and Close'
16. Continue with each product you want to add to your store.

Feel free to poke around in your Cartfly admin section to see the other aspects of your store. Once all of your products are added, you're ready for business!

LINK

www.cartfly.com

CafePress

CafePress is where people from all walks of life gather online to create, sell and buy a variety of "print on-demand" products with no upfront costs or inventory risk.

YOU CAN SELL

- Merchandise you design such as t-shirts, posters, mugs, bumper stickers
- Books printed on-demand
- Audio and Data CDs

TOP REASONS TO SELL ON CAFEPRESS

- Gives you a free online shop to promote your products
- Produces each item when ordered using unique print on demand technology
- Accepts many payment transactions including major credit cards
- Ships your products worldwide
- Manages all returns and exchanges
- Offers customer service via toll-free phone and email
- Sends you a monthly cheque for your earnings on sales

ALL SHOPS INCLUDE

- Ability to create and sell over 80 different products
- Books, music, CDs and more
- Reliable online shipping hosted on their servers
- Secure checkout and credit card payment processing
- Domestic and international shipping of your products
- Phone and email support
- Ability to list products in the CafePress.com Marketplace which receives millions of unique visitors
- Promotional tools to help drive more traffic to your shop

CHARGES

A basic shop is free, while a premium shop costs $4.99 per month. They offer a free trial for this service so you can poke around before you commit. A one-time payment of $59.95 is required for a full year's Premium Shop Subscription.

LINK

www.cafepress.com

DynaPortal

DynaPortal offers an integrated web software suite of over 50 easy-to-use web applications. This 'mix and match' and drag and drop system is similar to a kiddies' 'pick and mix' sweetie shop.

Choose from a wide assortment of the most popular content management, social networking, advertising, e-business, community, collaboration, e-commerce and mobile applications, all hosted and easy to use. Although some of their case study sites look busy and possibly too cluttered, others are stylishly executed. They have a lot on offer so it is little wonder that some of their users cram as much as possible into their sites.

HOW IT WORKS

Just decide which applications you require, enter your categories, and begin to publish information or provide web products or services. The CMS management requires no technical or web page design skills and, if you want a special branded template, they offer custom site designs. You just add graphics, categories and content.

TOP REASONS TO USE DYNAPORTAL
- Applications come delivered, ready to use and working together from the start
- They all basically operate the same way under a single log-in and are easy to learn and use
- Engineered to minimise site admin
- Manages a lot of information quickly
- No development fees therefore lower total cost of ownership

FEATURES
- Blog
- Classified advertising server
- Contact management
- Contest
- Community forum
- Directories and business guides

- E-business, E-commerce, E-mall, E-store or shopping cart
- Email list management and Email newsletter
- Events, reservations and scheduling
- Membership with user management
- Messaging
- Photo gallery
- Poll and surveys
- Promotion and coupon
- Rating and reviews
- Social networking

CHARGES

Price upon application. They do offer a free trial so explore extensively.

LINK

www.dynaportal.com

Etsy

This is the place to buy and sell all things handmade. The Etsy community spans the globe with buyers and sellers coming from more than 150 countries; so it's perfect for all the home industries and handmade craft and hobbyists.

ONLINE STORE

When you sign up to be a seller, you get your own easy-to-use online shop. You can customise it with a banner, fill out a profile and setup your shop policies. Etsy sellers can also participate in Alchemy; a feature that allows buyers to post requests for custom made items and allows sellers to bid on those requests.

When my son was a toddler I made all his clothes. I even made the cutest little undies for him and his cousins and an adorable bikini for my niece so I wish I knew about this site back then!

TOP REASONS TO SELL ON ETSY

- There's no HTML required
- Setting up shop is easy and takes only a few minutes
- Customise your shop with a banner, profile and shop policies
- Get your own URL, example: yourname.etsy.com

- Join a community of helpful, knowledgeable craft sellers
- Chat with other 'Etsians', share tips and marketing strategies
- Attend online workshops in their virtual labs

CHARGES

It costs 20 cents to list an item for four months. When your item sells, you'll pay a 3.5% transaction fee.

NOT ALLOWED

- Anything that doesn't fit in one of the three categories
- Handmade goods created by someone else
- Illegal or prohibited items

Etsy shoppers are looking for handmade goods, vintage items and craft supplies so you may be able to reach the ideal customer for your products when you sell on Etsy. I haven't tried it, but if you're 'crafty', give it a go.

LINK

Browse www.etsy.com/fees.php before you commit.

Ning

Ning is the social platform for the world's interests and passions online. With Ning, you can make your brand social, amplify a cause you're passionate about, or simply forge strong relationships with like-minded people.

TOP REASONS TO USE NING

- There's no HTML required
- Get your Ning Network up and running in minutes
- Connect people around your interest or passion
- Integrate your brand
- Templates and visual control

FEATURES

- Share your Ning Network or maintain a private circle.
- Automatic Twitter integration, email invitations, and branded media players will hook in new members.
- Run your own ads and earn 100% of the revenue.

- Choose from one of 50 distinct and unique themes or create your own design with custom CSS.
- Add tabs and sub-tabs to specific pages and external links via the Tab Manager feature.
- Define your own profile questions for incoming members. Members can customise their profile pages with their own design, choice of widgets and profile applications.
- Customise an advanced member search based on your Ning Network's unique profile questions, including location.
- Choose to make your Ning Network, public or private, for members only.
- Moderate members before they join.
- Moderate photos, videos, groups, chat and events before they're posted.
- You and your members can invite new members.
- Cross post Status updates on Twitter, and share content across the Internet with built in tools.
- Dynamic activity feed of everything happening across your Ning Network including status updates from members.
- RSS Feeds In and RSS Out, which pull in feeds from your blog, website or news source to create an ongoing stream of information.
- Enable your members to upload and share photos and videos.
- Automatically present your members with the option to embed your Ning Network's branded photo slideshows or video players anywhere on the web and link back to your Ning Network.
- Enable your members to see who's online and chat in real-time with the persistent chat feature across the bottom of your Ning Network or pop it out into its own window.
- Members can set up groups on your Ning Network with images, membership, comments and a discussion forum.
- Discussion forums add richness to your content. You can limit forum topic creation to you or open it up to all of your members.

- All members can post blogs. Display everyone's blog posts as a tab or just feature specific blog posts on your Ning Network's Main Page.
- Organise events and keep track of who is attending. Restrict event creation or open it up to all of your members.
- Further customise the experience on your Ning Network with additional features.

CHARGES
Prices start as low as $3 a month, which allows you to go ad-free.

LINK
www.ning.com

Sub Hub

SubHub membership software makes it easy to build a membership site and charge for access to premium content. They offer several ways to make money from advertising, affiliates or selling products and downloads.

TOP REASONS TO USE SUBHUB
- Quick and easy for you to build and manage
- Add images, streaming audio or video clips
- Font, layout and colours all manageable
- A website is built using a mix of different modules
- Manage from a CMS control panel

HOW TO MAKE MONEY WITH SUBHUB
- Charge for access to your own premium content, such as articles, a members-only forum, digital downloads, video and audio
- Charge for recurring subscriptions or memberships
- Add advertisements with Google AdSense and banner ads
- Set up your own SubHub store to sell products and downloads
- Charge for pay-per-view videos
- Promote offline events such as seminars, mentoring and consultancy

FEATURES

- Content
- Template design
- Forums
- Newsletters
- Member database
- Payment processing with PayPal, Authorize.net and Sage Pay/Protx payment gateways
- SubHub is PCI-DSS compliant

SEO

SubHub optimises your website to attract free search engine traffic. Every page is automatically optimised for search spiders, so new content is added quickly to search results.

HOSTING AND OTHER BITS

Like the other hosted sites mentioned above, SubHub also takes care of your hosting. This includes bandwidth, security, back-ups, maintenance, upgrades and your website is monitored 24/7 to ensure that it's always working properly.

CHARGES

Prices start from £49.97 per month and if you want a professional template designed, it will cost you a one off fee of £597. They also offer a free trial so you can get the feel of the editor and admin system. Have a play and then decide.

LINK

www.subhub.com

Yahoo

Yahoo! provides a complete turn-key solution for any vendor to offer e-commerce services.

TOP REASONS TO SELL ON YAHOO!

- Create a store with easy-to-use tools
- Use a wizard to add all your product details
- Accept credit, debit, and PayPal payments

- Drive traffic to your site with free marketing features and discounts
- Includes a grand opening email
- Easily process and ship orders
- Measure your success with extensive reporting capabilities

CHARGES

Fees start at $35.95 per month.

LINK

http://smallbusiness.yahoo.com/ecommerce/index.php

Instant Sites

When I say instant site, what I mean is pretty damn instant! An instant site is like having a website builder on hand to get your website made fast.

It is similar to a blog, in that all you have to do is pick a template, customise it to fit your brand and type of business, then hit the publish button. Some, though, won't be template based and come more as an 'out of the box' or 'off the shelf' website.

Pros:

- ✓ Fairly cheap and affordable
- ✓ Lots to choose from - surf for best options
- ✓ Quick and easy to get online
- ✓ Lots of nifty gadgets and buttons
- ✓ Huge time saver
- ✓ No HTML knowledge or coding needed
- ✓ Some integrate with other tools, such as Photoshop, Flash and eBay

Cons:

- ✗ Could be restricting because of template use
- ✗ Often no human support
- ✗ Extra features may require more cash outlay
- ✗ Check their rates if you need them to fix issues
- ✗ Some sites may be hard to use

Pay Monthly Sites

A pay monthly site gives you the benefit of having a bespoke or, at least, semi-bespoke site built for you. You then pay it off monthly, which of course includes the hosting. And the beauty is that you don't need any technical knowledge, you simply use theirs.

WHAT'S THE DIFFERENCE?

There isn't much difference between an Instant Site and a Pay Monthly site, except that some suppliers offer only an instant site, while others take their instant sites one step further and provide a bespoke service.

In other words, if you like one of their templates and monthly payment packages, yet you want a few tweaks, nips and tucks, you can ask them for a bespoke quote based on their pay monthly sites.

Many development companies have realised the value in offering cheap and affordable website design through a pay monthly scheme. This covers all aspects of creation, from a CMS site to a fully fuelled e-commerce site with shopping carts and SEO solutions.

While some work as a virtual 'website developer' and will give you a specially built site on a payment plan, others only give you a basic template option on a pay monthly plan.

EXPERIMENTAL

Mumsnet needed the advice of a developer to know what they could buy 'off the peg' and what needed to be built for them. Carrie Longton believes this only works if you trust the developer. There are so many more instant sites available now than there were when Mumsnet started, so if you don't know a developer and can't afford to pay one, then it's probably worth experimenting with instant sites first.

WYSIWYG EDITOR

Instant websites also provide next generation, browser-based WYSIWYG (What You See Is What You Get) applications for creating and editing websites. These text editors make it easy to create any style of website in minutes and to construct pages.

The following image shows how this page on my pay monthly site was created using the WYSIWYG editor. The layout I used for this page is a two column layout with a left sidebar.

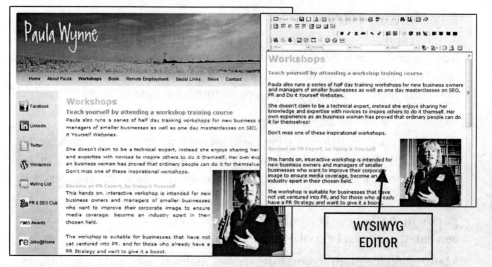

Some providers claim to have an easy 3-step or 5-step wizard to help you create, modify and update your own website without any technical HTML know-how.

With an instant website you can choose from ample design templates, customise your site with colours and your logo in your header, add pages and navigation menus, insert images, tables and add graphics. You won't need to buy hardware or software and most of the companies offer a vast range of features.

Must Haves

When researching the different companies who offer these sites, make sure you have a powerful admin section with site stats and SEO. Having a drag and drop facility may also make web-life easier.

MUST HAVE LIST

✓ CMS admin section	✓ Unlimited pages
✓ Site stats	✓ Site map
✓ SEO	✓ Contact forms
✓ Site wizard	✓ RSS Feed
✓ Editor (WYSIWYG)	✓ Insert tags

Your Features

Depending on the type of site you are planning, there are some essential features you need, so have a look at this list and decide what is important to your online business:

- If you're setting up a shop online you will need an easy E-Shop. Now may be a good time to revert back to your goals from Day 1 to see how your business aims to grow. Also, review your navigation map to see how many pages you need.

- Even if you don't intend to have many pages to start, I would definitely go for the unlimited page option if you are planning on a resource, magazine, community site or large product based site.

- Also, check if they allow unlimited products. You don't want to find you have chosen the wrong site or package a few months down the line. Way too painful!

- Taking payments with credit cards or PayPal is vital if you intend to sell products or services through your online business.

GIVE YOURSELF A BONUS

Bonus features could include:

- Blogger
- Forum
- Image gallery
- Feedback forms
- Polls and surveys
- Counter watch - a bit old fashioned now
- Guestbook, able to moderate comments

EXTRA, EXTRA, READ ALL ABOUT IT

Above all, your instant or pay monthly site should be easy and quick to use. Some provide a domain and free hosting as well as email pop box or email forwarding, such as 123 Reg. Check the small print and see if they will submit your site to search engines. No big deal if they don't, just one thing less for you to do.

CHOOSING AN INSTANT SITE

Google the word 'instant site' or 'pay monthly website' and see the plethora of links that come up. I've had a good look and there are some great looking options. Selecting one is entirely your choice.

However, I would suggest that you can afford to be choosy. Look at their own website and see what kind of image they are portraying.

The following screenshot shows the CMS interface in Lucent Vision's Pay Monthly Sites.

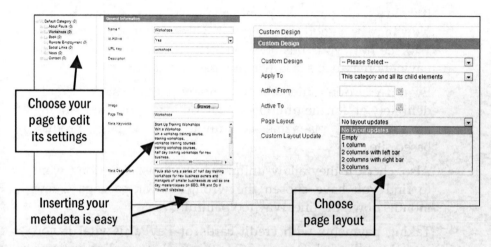

Choose your page to edit its settings

Inserting your metadata is easy

Choose page layout

If you want an up-market image or corporate image for your website, but the company you are browsing has clip art or loads of flashy gadgets giving you a headache then leave immediately. If you want something cheap and cheerful, test the various options before diving in. Go back to your planning and research, read your notes and remind yourself about your branding and navigation.

There are loads more to choose from. Google 'pay monthly websites', 'instant websites', 'hosted websites' and any other keywords to see the choice. I wanted to show you an example and I must admit, I didn't have much time to try more than one, but luckily this one came up smelling like roses.

LINK

www.lucentvision.co.uk

Instant Potholes

Okay, so if these instant sites are the next best thing since peanut butter, what is the down side?

Firstly, you have to stick to their templates and their so-called wizards. Check for 'extra' item costs as some sites have additional charges. If they do, have a good look at their rates and consider your budget if you anticipate you'll need those services in future.

The best ones will offer a tour and demo, so take it and spend time on a few sites that get your top vote.

Have all of that valuable information in front of you to be sure you are choosing the right site. And if you're not sure, call the company with any questions you have.

If they are worth their salt, they will give you a contact number and talk you through a possible instant site. I would also ask them if you can test their admin area so you can see for yourself how easy (or not) it is to use.

Consider this:

- What if you run into difficulty while choosing a template or customising your instant site?
- What if you can't upload your logo or have other technical issues and can't get hold of them?

If you're not happy with the answer then don't go there. It's not worth the hassle and downright pain you'll suffer.

BOTTOM LINE

If there is no contact number don't bother with them. Give a few suppliers a call and ask some pertinent questions to see how they respond and react. This will give you a gut feeling if they are worth your money or not.

Summary

We have covered a huge amount in the last couple of days, and I suspect the vision of your website is slowly taking shape. After discovering the difference between website software, a hosted website and a pay monthly site, you will no doubt have an idea of which one to choose.

Before you jump in though, read on to find out more about building a bespoke website and how to work with developers which, in itself, is an in-depth subject.

Checklist
- [ ] Choose a domain
- [ ] Decide between a blog site and website
- [ ] Check out hosted sites featured today
- [ ] Google for website software suppliers
- [ ] Research Pay Monthly Instant sites

Day 6: Bespoke Websites

Tailored Solutions

A bespoke site is one that is completely tailored to your needs, such as Remote Employment and Remote Worker Awards, which were built for our specific requirements. They can be expensive and time consuming to build and costs often run into hundreds of thousands, but there are great bespoke agencies out there who will cater for a much smaller budget.

Today you'll find out how to work with a developer and create a brief to ensure your website goes to plan. We also examine various options of working with developers and web design agencies with a full list of questions to ask when contacting potential developers.

> *"The word bespoke often gives the wrong impression, like it's a special indulgence or luxury having your website hand-crafted."*
> Clare Medden, Medden Design

The best advice here is to do your research. If you have a particular need with exact keywords, Google the keywords with the word 'software' after it. You may come up with developers who specifically design websites for your industry.

If not, use the keywords to have a good old nose around the net to see if there are sites you like that have a development company listed at the bottom. Call them up and ask for a quote - suitably armed with your navigation brief.

Pros:

 ✓ An ocean full of developers to choose from
 ✓ Saves your time setting up templates
 ✓ No HTML knowledge or coding needed
 ✓ New technical expertise used
 ✓ Use their skills to best advantage

✓ Ensure they are SEO experts and build your site with best optimisation methods
✓ Choose carefully – go for reputable and recommended developers
✓ Knowledge and experience in your sector can be useful
✓ Check out site ownership and copyright issues before signing – you should own it if you're paying for it!

Cons:

✗ Nifty gadgets, buttons and features cost extra
✗ Some developers can be very difficult to work with
✗ They can fool you with jargon and rip you off
✗ Unforeseen changes and features will often require extra cash outlay
✗ Beware cheap upfront costs and high ongoing 'maintenance' prices
✗ Watch that they don't claim ownership of your ideas, domain name, content or intellectual property
✗ Get a contract up front so you know where you stand and what you own
✗ Larger development companies often have so much work that they don't have time to keep up with new trends

Hosting

Hosting has once again reared its head, but for good reason. If you are going the bespoke development route you will need to find a hosting solution to match your site's needs.

However, most development agencies will provide this facility so I wouldn't worry about it now. Add it to your question list to see if they can host for you and how much they charge. Most will and it can make life a lot easier. Besides, you have so much else to do!

Intellectual Property

Before we discuss working with developers to create your own bespoke or specially built site, I want to quickly cover Intellectual Property Rights (IPR).

Basically an IPR lets people own the work they create. It could be the result from the creation of an idea, a brand, an invention, a design, a song or any intellectual creation, such as a website development or its design.

Intellectual Property can be owned, bought and sold, so ensure you own the rights to yours or you may come unstuck if you want to move to another development company down the line.

There are some horror stories of how entrepreneurs spent thousands only to find they don't own the site they paid for and cannot move it somewhere else. So do be aware of this risk and ask the question about who owns what up front.

My advice here is to get a free half hour or hour's consultation from a legal firm on IPR telling them what you intend to do with your site. Then, if this could be an issue, decide if you need to pay for further legal advice.

You should check who holds the IPR of the bespoke site that will be built for you. You *should* own it as you will be paying for it, but it isn't as easy and clear as that. That is why I suggest you get a contract or speak to a legal advisor on this hot and touchy subject.

If you pay for the logo, content and images, you own them. When it comes to the technical coding, you need to define exactly which files and code you own. Just because you have paid for a website, it doesn't mean all of the features are now yours. Sometimes the developer will use bits of software they've created to bolt onto your CMS system.

> **FOR EXAMPLE:** they will use a standard editor for you to change your pages. This will not be owned by you and the same goes for other similar items. Get a list in writing from the developer of what you will own and not own, before they begin work.

Thinking of Using a Developer?

A web developer is the person that designs and creates the code for a website. If they come from a marketing and design background, they usually know design and can be truly great at it. But for your site to be successful you *must* ensure they also optimise your website to perform well in the search engines.

Many, many web designers fall down and get SEO (Search Engine Optimisation) so wrong. My first and foremost caution is to ensure your developer knows about SEO and works with it to the point of advocating SEO and shouting from the roof tops that they are SEO kings.

In fact, them having SEO knowledge and foresight can make or break your website. I have heard this time and time again so I want to stress how important it is. It is easy to check; if they are good at SEO, sites they have built will come out on top of searches using the industry's keywords.

A stunning design will brand your online business and bring you creditability, but it won't drive traffic to your site. Our mistake, like so many other new businesses, was to get our website beautifully designed and then optimised *after* launch. Wrong.

Almost all sites will work best if they are built and created with optimisation as the main goal. If this rings alarm bells, don't worry, we can fix it. Read *Pimp My Site* to find out. A poorly optimised site can be repaired, but you may be in for a lot more work.

We talked about your navigation map a couple of days ago, and this is when it comes in to play once again. A properly designed navigation map or menu helps to ensure long term success and also gives your developer a damn good idea of what you want.

Karen Hanton set up TopTable with a bespoke site and her key to 'getting something good out at the other end' was to add as much information on the spec or web development brief as possible. She now has a team of in-house developers maintaining their busy site.

Their homepage offers more than a dozen ways to search and book a perfect meal out. We'll learn how to create a brief soon.

 CLARE MEDDEN ON DIY WEBSITES
If you find a DIY website interesting and fun, create your own. If you find it frustrating and confusing then pay a developer to do it and save a lot of stress and hair pulling.

Go it Alone or Develop a Developer

Using a developer can give your new website a huge jump to get online quicker, especially if you have specific requirements. Some developers though can be rude with insufficient customer services skills.

Mostly you will find that a small agency or one-person developer has the pros of being local and therefore easy to access, as well as being flexible in timescales for your site's build. The downside is that if they're busy you'll have to wait in line for their time.

A larger agency will often be more rigid with timings, making it harder to get to see someone. Plus lots of people to work with you may never ever meet your actual developer. The upside here is that you may find their rates more favourable, but not always as they could have higher overheads. If they are large they should have an impressive portfolio of work to back up their claimed expertise.

Due to the scores of people involved it should be quicker to get things done than your one person set up. However that could also lead to no one taking ownership or responsibility when errors raise their ugly heads.

> *"We initially used a friend who was a developer
> to do our site in return for equity."*
> Carrie Longton, Mumsnet

I have worked with both a small and larger agency and they both have their pros and cons. Essentially, you need to go with your gut instinct, but do your homework before you sign anything!

And don't be afraid to keep going back with more questions or anything that is bothering you. This is a huge decision and your final choice will make or break your website's success. If they get annoyed by too many questions and you haven't even started working with them, then imagine what it will be like when you are working with them and something goes wrong. Asking questions is a perfect way to assess their customer service skills.

Clare advises to first go it alone, especially if your website is small and growing. A website is never a fixed thing, it should continually evolve. Once you find you don't have the time or inclination to do it yourself then get a developer. By then you will have the skill-set to know if they are proficient enough to do a great job on it.

How To Work With a Developer

In most cases, using a professional web designer will ensure that you strengthen your website strategy. If you have chosen the best and most suitable web design agency then you can maximise their skills throughout your website.

Their experience in strategy development, idea generation, designer tools, implementation and even follow up evaluation should guide you through what could be a somewhat daunting and stressful time.

Consulting external advisers with specific design-related experience can also help you find the right designer. At one stage we almost went down this route and then decided against it as we preferred to learn as much as we could. Knowledge is power as they say, so learning about your site's needs, will help you in the long run.

From the outset you should tell the developer how 'hands on' or 'hands off' you want to be. Don't be scared of offending them if you don't like something. Get everything you want written into the contract and have set parameters for finish times, number of drafts and what happens if you don't like something.

KAREN HANTON ON SPECIFICATIONS...

When you think you've done the spec of what you want, go back and double the amount of detail! This is by far the most common reason for developers producing something you don't want.

How to Choose a Web Developer

Once you have a detailed and thorough navigation map or menu and a brief with all your branding ideas, you need to start looking for the right developer to work with.

A good way to start is to get referrals and recommendations from business colleagues. Consult your list of favourite sites and check the bottom of the page to see if the developer has a company name or link. If not, don't be afraid to approach the company and compliment them on their great site and then ask for the developer's contact details. You can also try Googling a developer who may work within your specific industry.

> **FOR EXAMPLE:** when we were looking to re-launch Remote Employment with the best job board software, we 'Googled' 'Job Board Software Developers', 'Job Board Web Designers', 'Job Board Web Developers' and found a multitude to contact.

Firstly, we asked all our main questions and then met them in person. This is vital to know if you can work with them, if they will help and support your ideas, how technical they are and if they are active search engine optimisers. We had learnt this latter lesson first time around so it was important for us to understand how they worked with optimisation and a face-to-face meeting did the trick.

Clare believes that artistic types will give you something visually stunning. Smooth salesmen will usually mean you pay more and get less. Friendly, open and approachable means you'll strike up a good relationship, and hopefully create the ideal website.

Find out how much work they currently have on – 'nothing' is a worrying answer! Ask them what websites they have worked on and contact their clients to get a recommendation. Pitch your project to many companies, then sift through the replies and find the ones that reassure you the most.

Don't just choose by price. You do get what you pay for, but websites can be as simple or complex as you want. No two developers will be quoting for exactly the same job, only their idea of what it entails. So the costs could differ widely. Some developers give 'Rolls Royce' quotes when all the client needs is a 'Ford'.

Baby Developers

Babyworld was established in 1999 and they are now working on creating a new site using a mixture of free software, such as Drupal, with developers who have expert technical knowledge of how to build websites from scratch.

Editor, Debbie Bird, says it is sometimes difficult when the creation's background does not always relate to the end product. While Debbie is focused on the structure and navigation of the site, and how it will look to the end user, often technical developers concentrate on complicated programming without any visual flair.

Debbie wants Babyworld to be based on a solid foundation and the smoothest way of getting visitors around the site. Like all things 'creative' she says that, although developers are open to individual experience and tastes, finding the right balance can be a delicate procedure.

Debbie feels that it helps to work with developers who have empathy with your subject. She agrees that you should examine other websites your potential developers have created, as it will give you a feel for their style and how they present the information.

> FOR EXAMPLE: The images used on Babyworld need to be sensitive in areas where having a baby has had complications and the members feelings need to be considered. It certainly is not appropriate to put images of pregnant women in an area of infertility or bereavement.

A good developer needs to understand your business and work with you to ensure your site compliments the information you are sharing.

Briefing A Developer

A web designer or developer's job is to come up with a specific website result that works for both of you, so it is important your brief outlines as much detail as possible

With Remote Employment, we agreed some initial stages with our developers. Most agencies will work along similar lines:

- **CONCEPT** – Their graphic designer will look at design concepts and ideas.
- **SPEC** – You will choose which design and final navigation gets developed.
- **DESIGN** – We had a first draft and made only a few changes before the final draft.
- **IMPLEMENTATION** – The build of your site before it goes live normally involves the techie bits, but you should be active in watching it evolve the way you have planned.
- **DEVELOPMENT** – This may need lots of tweaking and experimentation to get it right.
- **TESTING** - Your site will be on a development server so only you can see it and start to review and test every aspect.
- **SIGN OFF** – After testing they will require you to sign off the final version prior to making it publicly available.

Remember your SMART goals and apply the same principle to your objectives with your developer. Ensure that they understand what you aim to achieve with your new site and how quickly you want to achieve this.

Be Specific, ensure it is Measurable, how easily will it be Achieved, what Results you expect and when you anticipate them in exact Timings.

Have an idea of finances in mind. Don't ask what it will cost; instead explore what you can get for your budget.

Quoting is a tough task, as a developer rarely knows how complex the project really is. Clare suggests this leads to nearly all design companies over quoting when asked to give an estimate.

If you simply say, "I have £X in mind to spend on a website, what will that get me?" a trustworthy developer can quickly calculate how many hours work that buys you, and break it down into specific parts of the design process.

So don't be scared of starting with a small budget, then adding more and more features as the site evolves. Make sure you can add to your site at a later date and if so, how much the changes would cost.

Help A Developer With Your Brief

Be as specific as possible, without taking on the entire design yourself. You are paying someone to design your site, so it's counterproductive to employ them, and then do *their* job for them. Tell them which colours and styles you like, with lots of examples, and the keywords that sum up your idea of the site and its purpose. The more detail your brief holds, the quicker a developer will see your vision.

> *"Please be very careful about any license agreement you get into."*
> Polly Gowers, Everyclick

You want to try and get the designer on the same page as you, but let them use their experience of what works on successful websites to make your idea even better. A good designer should come back to you with mood boards or mock ups so you can check they are heading in the right direction. But if you dislike something they do, say so.

It's their job to design your site, and it should look how *you* want and plan it to be. A good designer will explain the reasons why they may have deviated from your brief. It's up to you to choose whether to incorporate these ideas or not.

Web Development Brief

Go back to your branding and navigation map and outline this and the other points mentioned above and add them into a Development Brief.

This will cover your website's key objectives, its short and long term goals and your company's strategic goals.

YOUR DEVELOPMENT BRIEF SHOULD INCLUDE

✓ Background – include your 'why me, why now' and a brief background of your anticipated customers or clients.

✓ Objectives – write a detailed summary of your aims, objectives and goals and how you aim to fulfil these.

✓ Branding – how you see the branded design, include the details we discussed earlier in your branding brief, even show a few hand drawn amateur desktop designs.

✓ SWOT – your strengths, weaknesses, opportunities and threats.

✓ Technical issues – list any techie questions you may have about things you don't understand. This is also the time to comment on any limitations you may have.

✓ Project management – include your budget and timeline, list your management team who may be involved in any or all of the review processes and how you will communicate with them.

✓ Intellectual Property (IPR) – it is vitally important that you establish who owns the intellectual property rights to the designs and development being produced.

✓ Evolve Your Brief – make changes as you speak to mentors, NEDs, team members, business colleagues, friends, family and other advisors. Add these new changes and discuss them with your development agency or keep them handy for future use if you're using a free website option.

✓ Navigation map – now may be a good time to take another look at your navigation menu and see if you have any further ideas to add.

POLLY GOWERS ON INSTANT SITES AND DEVELOPERS...

- **If you want to sell the website one day you have to own it all**

- **Having your site stuck on someone else's platform could restrict your business exit**

CMS Your Bespoke Site

We discussed a CMS (Content Management System) earlier to ensure you will be in control of updating your site's content. If the developer can't, or won't, provide CMS go somewhere else.

Ask the developer to show you some examples of the admin sections that they use and even see if you can have a little play with one for a few days. Don't be afraid to ask for this, if they believe in their system they will be happy to oblige!

Questions To Ask a Web Developer

Start making a note of pertinent questions to ask to make sure the web developer has the ability and competence to meet your website needs.

Now, draw up a list of 10 possible web developers by looking at their work and case studies. Before you approach them for quotes, you need to ensure your brief is complete. Also, outline the ideas and suggestions you need to explore in more detail and make a list of questions to ask.

The company's track record is key. Ask for some references and contact their clients. Be sure to enquire about the company's ability to solve problems - this is way more important than if their work appeals to you on an aesthetic level.

Meet with the designer and developer. You need to establish a rapport and start a good working relationship. This checklist is an amalgamation of our experts' advice.

Question Checklist

Initial Concept:

- ☐ Are they specialists in your sector?
- ☐ What is their confidentiality policy?
- ☐ Can you have a CMS?
- ☐ Is there access to a test admin section to explore how it works?
- ☐ How long will development take?
- ☐ Do they have similar projects?
- ☐ Are there any other timescales involved?
- ☐ Do they have standard contracts to avoid the cost of legal fees?

❑ Can they give you references for other client sites? You want names and contact details to call and discuss their service with their other clients.

Design:

❑ Will you be included in brainstorming sessions?
❑ Will you own the IPR on the logo?
❑ Who owns the Intellectual Property and copyright?
❑ When will you get the initial designs?
❑ How long will it take to revise them?
❑ What if you don't like the designs?
❑ Do you get a breadcrumbs trail? It may not be necessary now, but could be helpful in future. See the section on breadcrumbs in the Branding chapter.

Implementation:

❑ When will they fit your site design and build into their schedule?
❑ How long will the first draft take?
❑ How can you remain in control of the overall process?
❑ Are they SEO experts?
❑ Will your site have all the vital SEO architecture built in?
❑ Do they offer any guarantees?
❑ Will there be regular progress reviews to keep you up to date?
❑ Can they outline review stages?
❑ Who owns the coding IP? Be sure to understand what you own and what you don't own.
❑ Can they meet your launch date? Will they guarantee this?

Testing:

❑ How long is the testing period?
❑ Do they provide hosting? And is it included in the cost?
❑ What happens if the site does not meet deadlines?
❑ Although you trust your designers to use their own skills and judgement, what measures are in place for critiques?
❑ How should you point your domain to their servers? You can either give them access or ask them how to do it.

KEEP CONTROL
Don't let them buy the domain in case it goes pear shaped and they won't release the domain when your site is successful.

Sign Off and Go Live:
- ❑ When do you expect to go live?
- ❑ Who will sort out the server?
- ❑ What happens if your site gets so big it keeps crashing?
- ❑ If so, will they supply a dedicated server?
- ❑ What will that cost?
- ❑ Can they provide regular backups?
- ❑ What happens in the event of a crash or downtime?
- ❑ What if you want to transfer the site or host it elsewhere?

Payment:
- ❑ What do they charge?
- ❑ Is there a fixed rate for the job?
- ❑ What about extras?
- ❑ How do they expect to be paid?
- ❑ What happens if you pay late? Beware of this as they may hold you to ransom.
- ❑ What happens if they don't deliver the full brief?

Payment Plan

Once you have all the final developer quotes, go through your budget and formulate a payment plan that you can offer the developer. Feel free to negotiate excellent terms for your development costs and push them to their limit. Don't give in to upfront payments, instead spread it out over the time of the site build and even after your site is live, possibly to the extent of a couple of months after your go live date.

This way you get the benefit of holding onto your money for as long as you can and you retain a small semblance of control if they don't deliver what is promised. It also gives you a leverage tool if there are any issues after it goes live. One lady at a speaking event I delivered told me she gave a company £2,000 for a full payment on her site and when she didn't like the logo, they refused to give her money back.

Other small issues led to friction and she was so distraught, she preferred to lose her money rather than argue over a logo.

If the developer won't agree to your payment proposal, discuss alternatives and suggest a deposit on first design spec. Be firm and don't let them push you around. Remember that they need your business as much, if not more, than you need their skills!

Clare has pointed out that lots of developers ask for a large deposit, because so many people start a project and unfortunately don't see it through. She said it isn't because they are after your money, but simply because they have to cover their time if the project doesn't complete.

You could confirm a deposit, another payment after 1st draft and then one final payment on completion, i.e. once testing has been successfully concluded.

Dealing With Developer Issues

Issues will arise, which is why it's important to have a good relationship with your developer, so you can speak to them openly.

Clare suggests that if it feels like you are fighting in opposite directions you should ask them why they are taking a particular route, when you specified something different in the brief. The answer should validate their decision. Or get them to re-evaluate their choice. Hold back full payment until you are 100% happy.

Summary

Today we explored the option of creating a website with your own design and functionality. If you go this route you need to establish the IPR ownership of your new website. We also talked about how to find a developer to create this new wonder and more importantly, how to work with them and ensure your fingers don't get burnt.

There are some exciting days ahead as we start to populate your site with content and find ways to earn money. So, if you can take the pace, let's move on...

Checklist

- ❑ Research development companies
- ❑ List developer questions
- ❑ Create a website brief
- ❑ Formulate a payment plan

Day 7: Content

Sticky Content

The term 'Sticky Content' refers to ensuring your visitors stick when they land on your site pages, like a fly that fastens onto a sticky fly trap.

Not a nice image I know, but for long term success it is vital that your site's content should make browsers stick and stay. Okay, maybe they won't set up camp and live on your site, but you want to ensure they keep coming back. The way to do this is to always have fresh, topical, dynamic content. Content includes text, articles, data, member or user profiles, reviews, feeds, jobs, news, products, merchandise tables, visual and creative graphics, images and animations as well as audio and video files.

Today we will cover all aspects of content and this covers what to feature, what not to feature, where to get content, how to keep people coming back to you site again and again. Get them recommending the site to others. This is all crucial to building and maintaining your traffic.

SO YOU'RE A PUBLISHER NOW

Every time you post content on your website you are publishing it, so in effect you have become a Publisher. Your content is a valuable asset, which deserves the same care and attention that a magazine publisher or newspaper editor will place on *their* content.

Your Content Strategy should focus on your goals and objectives for your site as well as fulfilling your target audience or niche visitor's needs.

"People love to see their own stuff on the web.
This can create huge amounts of content quickly."
Karen Hanton, Toptable

Your web content must resonate with your visitors and do more than just sell your products or services. It must also contribute to your brand's positive image. Your carefully selected content aims to label your online business as a trusted industry source, so it should reflect your brand values and position you as a thought leader and sector expert. As you learn more about your audience and your site grows, so will your confidence as a publisher.

ASK YOURSELF THE FOLLOWING QUESTIONS

- ❏ What motivates my audience?
- ❏ What issues do they need to solve?
- ❏ What content and offer will induce them to purchase?
- ❏ How do they think and feel about my product?
- ❏ Why will they need my service?
- ❏ What benefits will it give them?
- ❏ How would I search if I were in their shoes?
- ❏ What product or offering will excite them the most?

Visibility = Credibility

We chatted briefly about an 'About Us' and 'Contact Us' page when we designed your Navigation Map.

One small area of content is your 'About Us' page where you get the chance to tell people about you and your products and more importantly, why they have to have them. You know that old 'to die for' expression? Use it here.

Don't wax lyrical and go overboard, just write out a fabulous summary with your unique proposal. Another important point to take on board is to let your personality shine. Don't be shy and hide who you are. You will build trust and creditability by showing yourself, your staff and founders.

"When starting out, use contacts to generate interest. It's obvious, but you need users to make any site work."
Carrie Longton, Mumsnet

We didn't include this when we first launched Remote Employment, thinking no one would care. Well, they did. We got so many emails asking more about us and then, when we added our contact number, the phone rang off the hook because people were interested to know more about us and talk to us.

When we added pages on ourselves as Founders and then followed that up with a 'team' page, our visitors were delighted to meet us 'virtually' and we are constantly swamped with people telling us how wonderful it is to see the people behind the site. We are proud to show off our company's personality. You should be too. Being open and visible gains your visitors' trust and builds integrity.

Another option is to include a Google Map flagging where you are in the world so people know you really do exist. This is especially important if you have an office, warehouse or store where they can purchase goods.

Don't Hide Behind Logins

When we first started Remote Employment we thought we were clever to hide our jobs behind a login area so we could build up a member base.

This was a great idea for a while, as we did certainly build the database because visitors wanted to see what kind of remote and home working jobs we had on our site. When they logged in they found a smorgasbord of tasty home working, remote working and home business treats.

But can you see the stumbling block? By not showing our job content openly, we were, in effect, telling the search engines not to search and index those most important areas.

> *"Original content is best so get your users involved.*
> *Case in point – Facebook."*
> Polly Gowers, Everyclick

We realised all too quickly the mistake we had made and it took many more months before we could rectify this. We moved to an 'open plan' solution to give everyone access to *all* our jobs and therefore resolve the sticky content issue - and give Google access to crawl all over our job content. Our solution was to ensure the job postings were public and then encourage people to register to *apply* for the jobs. Read *Pimp My Site* to see how we solved this issue (short and long term) and eventually became Google's No. 1.

Bounce Rate

Your bounce rate is affected by your content. You will see in your Google Analytics account (coming up) that you have a statistic called Bounce Rate. This is also termed as the Exit Rate (not to be confused by Exit Route as discussed earlier).

A Bounce Rate reflects the percentage of visitors who 'bounce away' to a different site, rather than continue on to your other pages. This happens when a new visitor only views a single page on your website and leaves without viewing any of your other pages. In effect they land, take a quick glance around and think, 'Mmm, not for me' and off they go again, like a flea bouncing around in a dog parlour.

GOOGLE'S DEFINITION: a bounce rate is the percentage of single-page visits or visits in which the person left your site from the entrance (landing) page.

They use this metric to measure visit quality. A high bounce rate generally indicates that site entrance pages aren't relevant to your visitors. This should remind you of our discussion a few days ago about your home page being crucial to spell out your key message.

Keep 'Em Coming Back

The more compelling your key landing pages, the more visitors will stay on your site, have a look around and convert to sales.

You can reduce your bounce rate by adapting landing pages to each keyword, link or advert that you run. Landing pages should provide the information, product or services mentioned in the original place where the visitor first spotted your link.

If you have different aspects to your site, ensure that the landing page links you give out are relevant to the page content. Another instance of being tacky and sticky is to ensure you have *enough* content.

> **FOR EXAMPLE:** when we first started out we had only a few jobs. It was like having a nice shiny new restaurant and nobody eating in it.

So we had to source loads of good remote and home working jobs as our content, to ensure we retained the stickiness on site to keep people viewing all our pages.

"Reward people for buying your product.
Keep it simple and make sure they have a
low threshold to 'get' something."
Karen Hanton, TopTable

Jobs are only one part of our content, in fact we didn't consider our jobs to be content at first, but quickly realised that they formed an integral part of our site content, along with resources and articles.

Loyalty Campaigns

Babyworld members return to the site for competitions, writing their pregnancy diaries, posting pictures of their babies, to ask and share advice and, of course, to interact with the community.

POLLY GOWERS ON CUSTOMER LOYALTY...

- **Build a great site with a unique proposition**
- **Encourage people to show your content on Facebook and Twitter**

Ask yourself why you go back to sites that you like. It is usually because it solves a problem or fulfils a need, it entertains you or it's offering the advice and support you need at a particular time in your life.

Debbie Bird believes websites are like people; some you like and some you don't. You can't be friends with *everyone* in the world!

You need to continually provide your audience with enticing offers, discounts, useful content and information of new products and new innovations. If visitors have registered with your site the easiest and most cost effective way to do this is via email marketing. Jon Buxton tracks the responsiveness of Babyworld's mail shots and tries different offers to see what works best for their readers.

User Generated Content

A great new way to increase stickiness and drive revenue is to offer your users the chance to add content to your site. This 'user-generated content' is a popular and easy, yet extremely powerful way to fill your site with valuable content and you could possibly earn revenue at the same time.

See a good example I created for my second book, *Pimp My Site*, at www.pimpmysiteclub.com. This site will showcase all the people who have read my books and created a successful website as a result. Pimp My Site Club will be user generated where you and others can register and link up with other new start ups in the same boat as you.

Essentially it will be a community of new website owners who want to connect with other start ups and need to stay in touch with experts in the industry, such as the ones in this book. You will have access to articles and templates for creating a great looking site and getting it to the top of the Google ladder. As a 'case study' you can 'pitch' your site to the media through the publicity club.

Set Up Dialogue

Communicate your key message by setting up a dialogue with your customers, clients and visitors. Think about having a little area that shares what's new and what's in store for anyone who visits the site for the first time. Hook them in and don't let go. Keep up the conversation with regular updates, but don't fall into the trap of having out of date info or, worse still, a statement with an actual date that is so old that it instantly ages your site!

How many times have you landed on a site and found that it was last updated years ago? Your immediate thoughts are: Is this site still relevant? Is anyone home? Are they out for lunch or has the business folded? You probably bounced away before finding out.

"Don't underestimate the amount of time it will take you to write copy, search for images and create web pages for your site."
Debbie Bird, Babyworld

Don't build up this wonderful new baby of yours, get it to the toddler stage and then abandon it. All your hard work should pay off when you keep it invigorated by updating information and adding relevant content as your website matures.

Any offers that have expired must be removed. Polls too, keep an eye on them. I remember adding a poll about the snowy weather and how it proved beneficial to home based workers, only to find it was still up there long after the snow had melted and people had forgotten the long weeks of blizzards. We all get super busy and juggle so many jobs so make a diary note so you don't forget these little things.

Better still, add a reminder in Outlook and even get it to send you an email reminder to change your poll or reader offers. We'll learn more about this later, but bear in mind that Google and other search engines favour sites that keep updating and adding new content. In *Pimp My Site* you'll see how we overcame our login issue and used articles on the site to increase our race up the Google ladder.

Meet The Parents

Mumsnet is a great example of how content can grow a site to become one of the top parenting sites in the UK. It has grown to over a million unique visitors a month.

Initially, it was a product review site with a discussion board.

It still is, but the discussion area is now the heart of the site with over 20 million page impressions a month. They also have blogs, recipes, a campaigns arm and editorial content – mostly based on user generated content. When online ad revenues took a dive, they took content offline and did a deal with Mothercare whereby they distributed a magazine of their reviews to Mothercare's customer base and Mumsnet sold advertising space.

Carrie's not sure it benefited the site, but believes it forced them to make sure the reviews were up to date. All in all, it kept them afloat in down times. Since then, their income sources have also evolved. Advertising is still the primary income source, but they also generate income from market research and consultancy. And, offline, they have a six book deal with Bloomsbury.

What a way to go! You too can be the next Mumsnet if you believe in your product and evolve with your site by constantly looking at ways to grow your content.

Headline Act

One way to ensure visitors don't bounce away merrily looking for somewhere juicier to land is to write snappy headings and sub headings. Here are some top tips...

POSITION IS KEY

Make sure your headlines are at the top of the page and not lost or crowded out by other 'stuff'.

INCLUDE KEYWORDS IN YOUR HEADLINES

Good use of your keywords can lead their eyes onto the next paragraph and get them reading your content.

DON'T ADVERTISE

Instead of 'selling' to your audience, make your headlines friendly. Also, rather than throwing 'sales talk' at your audience, give them valuable content to read and digest.

ALWAYS SHOW OFF THE BENEFITS

Instead of harping on about how good you are, tell your visitors what benefits they get from your products, services and website.

EASY TO READ

Don't use long, fancy highfalutin words. Use everyday terms with short, catchy phrases.

SHOW DON'T TELL

Keep your sub headings as sharp as your headlines. Think of sites that you like and look at their headline and sub headings. Remember, people scan read so sub headings should grab attention too.

Fresh and Topical

Sticky content is also largely affected by the amount of fresh and new content on your site and its relevance to your audience. Go back to your Navigation Map and recall what you want visitors to do when they hit your site. Good content will ensure you turn those hits into sales, repeat visitors or customers.

My top tip on page layout is to keep it clean and spacious with lots of white space and no headache-inducing clutter. You know what I mean by this, I am sure you have been onto sites that try and cram everything they can into a page and they think they're clever by using lots of different fonts and colours, yet all they're doing is giving you an instant headache. Bounce!

REMEMBER THESE PAGE LAYOUT GOLDEN RULES
- Use sub headings
- Use bullets
- Break up paragraphs
- Use web fonts: Arial, Times New Roman, Verdana
- Be clear about your page goals
- Update little and often - in bite size chunks
- Images facing into the page

CONTENT GOLDEN RULES
- Keep it visual, and not cluttered
- New pages and content bring visitors back
- Use shorter pages; viewers don't like to scroll down too far
- Don't use too much flashy animations and clip art
- Think carefully before adding background music
- Don't use pop ups - most people hate them and block them
- Utilise white space, don't overcrowd
- Stick to between 200 and 250 words if possible
- Add a call to action

PARAGRAPH TIPS
- Keyword-rich content is key
- People scan read so be aware of this
- Highlight key information
- Use punchy phrases
- Keep it simple
- Keep it short, sharp and snappy; no long rambling pages allowed
- Use definite and clear statements
- Fonts shouldn't be too small or too large, 8 to 12 point is good enough
- Ask and answer questions

157

- ❑ Grammar and spell check is so, so important for credibility
- ❑ Break up paragraphs - aim for a maximum of 4 sentences
- ❑ Vary sentence length, but lean on the briefer side
- ❑ Have a logical sequence to paragraphs

The 'F' Word

Okay, so I only used that sub heading to grab your attention and make sure you're still awake, I don't actually want you to use a 'Ramsay'!

Instead try something that's called the 'F Movement', which is how your eye moves across a web page. People scan across the top, from the left to the right, then immediately back down to the left. Most viewers will scan down the left hand side, picking up keywords or headers, while some people read to the bottom and flick their eye across to the right in the middle of the page. Thus creating an 'F'.

There have been many eye tracking studies done and you may have heard some experts call this the 'E Eye Scan'. Whatever you want to call it, it helps to keep this in mind when laying out your page content. The same goes for reading search result pages in Google.

Dyna-mums

Reviews can be another way to add content to your site. When Mumsnet started this feature it was labour intensive. As they reached larger numbers, they had to amend the way they did reviews. They now have lots of dynamic content, which is about 95% of the site, and most of this is user generated.

"Work out how you'll cope, moderate and edit content if you hit large scale."
Carrie Longton, Mumsnet

This echoes Karen Hanton's comments on how users love to have the opportunity to contribute and see their content published. By involving customers who use your site or service, you should never have any problem in generating new, dynamic content.

Karen advises you to enable people to upload images, which are edited and controlled. Toptable offer this facility and each restaurant's microsite features photos, 360-degree video tours, a map, description, party and group booking information, special offers and guidance on menu choices as well as a link to full menus for every meal.

Sources of Good Info

There are various ways to introduce good sticky content into your site. Depending on your audience, the type of site you have, and what image or brand you want to maintain, you can implement various forms of content.

TRY SOME OF THESE EXAMPLES

- Competitions, reader offers and give aways
- Games, daily quotes, chatty jokes, history dates
- Guides, directories, maps and weather
- Message boards, forums and chat rooms
- News, latest headlines, industry topics, articles
- Expert tips, advice, facts and figures

So, when you find information you would like to use, ask the owner of the site if you can link to them and use some of their articles. By doing so, give them a link and credit. Don't use it without asking for permission first!

The moral of the story here is to treat other sites as you want them to treat yours. You wouldn't want your articles used without you knowing and receiving a credit, so don't do the same before asking permission and providing the credit and link back.

What's New Pussycat?

As new ideas, products and services are the lifeblood of a business, the same goes for new content and a website. Google's creepy crawlers love sniffing out new articles, content and pages so give them the pleasure and make a diary note to add at least one new page each week. It could be an article, a blog, an offer, a product, a new service or just a plain page spiced with new keywords.

Depending on what your site is going to be, think very carefully about how you add new content that is topical to your audience. You will need to make sure that you have the resource available for the work involved in keeping it up-to-date and relevant. It all comes back to planning and knowing what you want your site to do.

*"Let genuine content drive your site
and bring you natural business."*
Clare Medden, Medden Design

Debbie Bird advises you to be careful when adding a new section to your site; think through the section, its headings and the maintenance of the section. A news or features section online needs to be up-to-date and easy to navigate. News sites link relevant pages together with statements such as 'other readers were interested in this topic.', but be sure you can maintain this style if you introduce it to your site.

Wrong Turn

Debbie goes on to say that her 'wrong turn' was not communicating with her members before changing a valued and established service that the site offered. The Antenatal Clubs had been established for nearly 11 years and members used them to keep in touch with their friends who they met when they were pregnant.

Babyworld wanted to change the setup to offer a paid-for expert advice service and antenatal classes. The mistake they made was to implement the change without speaking to the people that were using the service.

In the end they did listen to the members and have now set up a two tiered system where members can join any antenatal club for free and then, if they want the expert advice, they can pay and join the antenatal classes. The biggest lesson they learnt: never underestimate what members of your site want. Keep talking to them and asking for their views; even if you can't always accommodate what they want they appreciate the communication.

Audience Content

Scan your notes and research on your target audience to ensure you have met all the objectives for providing them with relevant and appealing content.

Research other sites and see the different ways they present theirs. Many times in this book we cover the theme 'Know Your Audience' and again, this is vital here. If you don't know and understand their requirements, how will you be able to fulfil their needs with sticky content?

Here's an example of a Toptable venue micro site, which gives you a snapshot of the restaurant with a 360 degree image, rating and reviews, promotions and online booking.

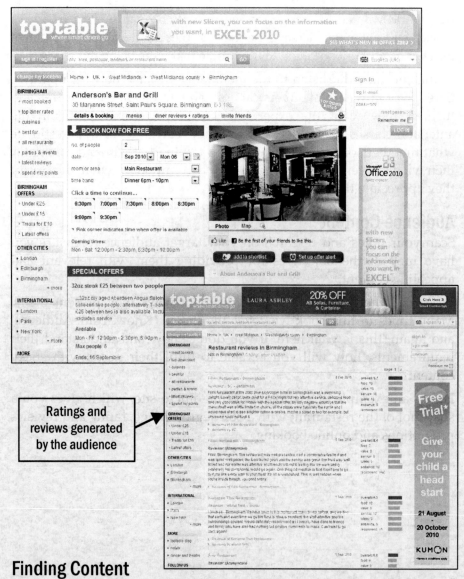

Ratings and reviews generated by the audience

Finding Content

Content is not difficult to obtain if you have a budget and can afford writers. However, while freelance writers are beneficial, they can be costly and, if you are just setting up, your funds may be limited. Register with public relations and news sites, where you can list your interests and receive relevant email updates about news stories and other events that are happening in your field.

DEBBIE'S EXAMPLES

- www.directnews.co.uk
- www.adfero.co.uk
- www.fingertipstv.com
- www.responsesource.com/index_journalist.php

PR companies often send out generic press releases and, depending on your type of site, they may have content that you can use.

For the Babyworld site it is difficult to simply just post up a press release as this would have also gone to all their competitors. Debbie will not duplicate information on Babyworld that appears exactly the same on another site.

Many PR companies will be accommodating in writing something unique for your site, as long as you give some publicity to their product or service. Contact the PR Manager and see if they will do this for you.

It can be a delicate balance obtaining content this way. You do need to be careful that you are not making the article an advertorial, as opposed to relevant and valuable editorial content your visitors will love.

ADVERTORIAL

An advertorial is an advert written in the form of an article, and presented in a way that makes it look like a news story, but is really written as a promotional feature rather than an impartial view point. Editorial is far more powerful content than advertorial, so steer clear of overtly biased info if you can.

Have a go at writing articles yourself. If possible, use your own knowledge to research the subject properly. You know your business, product or service better than anyone.

If your website is on a specialist topic try contacting charities or professional organisations to see if they will work with you in providing content in exchange for a link to their website.

FOR EXAMPLE: if you are an exceptional knitter and want to do something special with your hobby and make a difference to other people's lives, your website could help children to become more aware of creating handmade goods. So, you may want to match up with a kiddies charity for a special event teaching children to knit or a mara-knit-athon for young people with co-ordination difficulties.

Always make sure your content is relevant to your site and the overall subject you are focusing on. Don't be tempted to use copy that is interesting to you, but not relevant to your intended audience.

Article Content

Another content solution is to use articles from the large source of writers and internet marketers who want to create awareness for their product or service and drive back links to their sites. You also get to do this when marketing your site, however, as we now explore ways to find content, you can use article syndication sites to supply you with fresh, high-quality, hot-off-the-press content.

Sign up to for an article distribution account; some are free, and they'll send you a regular stream of top quality articles on any or all of the following category areas:

- Arts & Entertainment
- Automotive
- Business - General
- Computers & Technology
- Finance & Investment
- Food & Drink
- Health & Fitness
- Home & Family
- Internet Marketing or Online Business
- Legal
- Pets & Animals
- Politics & Government
- Reference & Education
- Religion & Faith
- Self-Improvement or Motivation
- Social
- Sports & Recreation
- Travel & Leisure
- Writing & Speaking

A PUBLISHER ACCOUNT WILL ALLOW YOU TO

- Receive content related to your site
- Specify which categories you wish to receive articles from
- Set a daily limit on the number of articles you want to receive
- Or receive unlimited articles
- Approve new content automatically or manually

Remember to always credit the writer of the article you add to your site. Soon, you will be writing articles to promote your site and you will earn credibility, become an industry expert, help other website owners to create content and receive traffic back to your site. Article writing is twofold - so give and receive.

Google 'Article Syndication', 'Article Writing', 'News Syndication' or a combination of these words and you will find loads of sites to check out.

SOME TO TRY

- Free and Easy Sign up at Articles Base: www.articlesbase.com
- Affordable news and data feeds: www.allheadlinenews.com
- Tailored News Feeds: www.directnews.co.uk
- Comprehensive list of article distribution sites: www.articlepr.com
- High quality articles for publishers: www.submityourarticle.com
- A List Apart: www.alistapart.com/feed
- News Gator: www.newsgator.com/Individuals/FeedDemon/Default.aspx

You can also search article directories such as www.ezinearticles.com, www.goarticles.com and www.ideamarketers.com.

ARTICLE LINKING

There are loads of sites where you can write an article and submit it to their site, which in essence provides a link back to *your* site.

FOR EXAMPLE: if you make beautiful crafts you may want to share some secrets or specialist advice on your site and turn it into an article distributed to other sites. Use keywords in the text to link back to certain pages on your site.

You can also trawl article sites and then ask the author's permission to use their editorial.

Give the article writer a credit, as well as a link to their site and they should be happy enough to share it with you.

The same applies to you. If you write a cracking article and submit it to an article farm, you too can gain links back to your site by giving others permission to use it. Another time-hoover, so consider your priorities. If you get into this and find it fun then read the section on article marketing in *Pimp My Site*.

Dynamic Content

As the Internet is primarily information-driven, visitors are always searching for something. The most successful websites supply this demand with an RSS feed.

In the branding chapter we discovered that dynamic content is pages that are updated automatically, with little intervention from you.

Article Syndication Sites supply you with free website content that's continuously updated from a stream of article writers (you will join this group when you start marketing your site) who regularly write high quality, informative free reprint articles ready for your website.

BENEFITS OF FREE CONTENT FEEDS

- The more relevant content your site contains, the more traffic your site receives
- Sites that contain regularly updated information tend to be indexed more regularly by Google and other search engines
- Achieve a higher page rank because they deem you as important based on quality content
- By providing regularly updated information, your web site achieves a higher perceived value in the minds of your visitors - who then want to return to your site again and again
- This is one of the easiest ways to ensure your web site always displays fresh, quality content

Freebies

Let's face it, we all *love* freebies and give aways! So why not offer free stuff to your visitors? This can be in the form of offers and prizes from partner sites or you can give them a choice of free downloads. Either way, it works as an addition to your content and all the while incentivises people to sign up and share your website - a viral marketing tool.

Including a competition on your site also gives you the chance to gather data about your users and start building long term relationships with them. Be careful not to bombard them with junk mail, though, as the relationship will die a quick and sudden death.

One last thing on freebies: it can be a time consuming task sourcing offers and giveaways so only go this route if you have resources in place or know loads of free supplier offers.

Industry Expert

To become an industry expert you need to research your specialist sector. Debbie encounters many small parenting websites approach saying things like, "we are the biggest online with 600 members." 600 members is obviously not enough to make their statement of being "the biggest" true and makes the owners look silly.

Be careful about your statements. Be honest, but don't *think* you are the biggest, *know* you are the biggest! Get the figures behind you, know who else is doing what you are doing, and how well they are doing it.

> *"Anyone can become an industry expert by talking and listening to their customers."*
> Max Benson, MBE everywoman

If you get the research, planning and foundation right for your website it will grow and develop. Nurture your website as you would a child; plan its day, feed it with information and keep it clean and tidy.

Forums

Chat Rooms once conjured up images of a seedy place for underworld surfers to gather. As they've evolved, chat rooms now bring a sense of community to the word Forum. They are built for online discussions amongst different interest groups where people exchange messages and participate in conversations. Check to see if there are any forums on your chosen area of speciality and if not, consider starting a forum on your site.

FORUM JARGON
- Forums: The subject areas of discussion
- Boards: The specific subjects
- Topics: The comments and threads

How Forums Work

Most forums allow all visitors to view the forum, post a new topic and reply to other posts.

Some only allow unregistered guests to view posts, but they cannot reply or post a new topic until they have registered.

Others are completely closed so only invited registered users can see topics or posts.

> *"Our forum is the heart of our site!"*
> Carrie Longton, Mumsnet

The best way to run your forum is allow everyone to *see* posts but require that they register to reply to them. This way you bring traffic to your site with visibility of the subjects discussed and you gain new members by allowing them to reply to posts if they register.

Forum Moderator

As a Forum Moderator, you can access the admin section to manage the forum. You will be able to set up other Administrators, set rules and etiquette as well as 'bad word' lists, create or delete posts, threads and ban members who don't adhere to your forum rules.

As well as building content, forums can be used as a means to drive traffic to your site. You should be joining other forums related to your subject and posting comments about your site.

A forum is great as a topical area where members will use lots of keywords that are great fodder for search engines. It is a dynamic and 'always-changing' environment, so Google will visit and see that you have an active and relevant environment to your site.

168

However, do make sure you have a site that will be supported. There is nothing worse than visiting a forum that is not used. If you have a successful forum then find individuals who are prepared to moderate the forum for you.

It can be time consuming keeping a check on people and the posts that are being made. You don't want to suppress views being aired, but there are 'netiquette' rules for forums and you will need to manage that.

> *"Building a membership is all about the community and members come first - never deviate from that."*
> Max Benson, MBE, everywoman

Question yourself whether you really need a forum. Just because you can, doesn't mean you should create one.

Summary

Even though we started the day with visions of flies stuck on gooey fly traps, you now know how to ensure your new site wows your visitors with relevant and sticky content and keeps them interested and engaged.

We discovered that good quality content is the lifeblood of your online business as regularly updated content keeps your site fresh and alive. At the same time it keeps the search engines coming back to crawl your site and it becomes a traffic builder.

We also learnt some important lessons from our group of experts on how to ensure your visitors stick and stay, and then come back to get stuck all over again.

I'll never forget the time I once had to rush my son to the doctor and I came home to find that I had forgotten his school sandwiches, half smeared with peanut butter, on the kitchen counter. At the time I lived in a Nature Reserve which had all the benefits of a lovely lifestyle, but the reserve was also inhabited by monkeys.

Needless to say, the scamps had found their way in and I was cleaning peanut butter paw-prints off my kitchen counters and cupboards for days to come. The moral of the story: be like flies or monkeys and get sticky, get *really* sticky!

Checklist

- ❑ Are you going to have a member login area?
- ❑ Remember to check out your bounce rate in Google when your site goes live
- ❑ What content will you use?
- ❑ Find articles and content to include
- ❑ Find sources of good information
- ❑ Consider forums and chat rooms

Day 8: E-commerce

What is E-commerce?

Electronic Commerce, aptly named E-commerce, is the term used for the wide range of online facilities covering both business services and consumer products. Fondly known as Online Shopping, e-commerce is the exchange of a product or service in return for cash or goods. E-commerce has blossomed and grown over the past few years and, when this book goes to print, I am sure more new revolutions will have sprouted.

We are all aware of being cautious with secure data transference, especially where it concerns our banking details. and, luckily, so are the banks. They are constantly coming up with new methods to ensure there are no leaks in the system so we can all shop merrily on the cyber high street.

Today we are going to talk about various options for earning revenue from your website and investigate the best secure solutions for your online shop or electronic service.

Like the other areas we have covered so far, e-commerce needs to be researched, carefully planned and executed securely. If you're running an online shop, the easiest way to get started is to use easy selling solutions with secure hosted providers such as PayPal and Google Checkout. Or you can set up a first class e-commerce solution from scratch.

POLLY GOWERS ON ECOMMERCE...
The customer is king. Make sure their online journey is exemplary.

These organisations take the headache out of providing online security for your website, but they do take a percentage of the revenue you earn. The best way is to start small so you get familiar with their processes.

Have a look at a few sites that do this well and buy something from them to learn how the good websites trade online.

JON'S EXAMPLES

- www.amazon.co.uk
- www.iwantoneofthose.com
- www.wiggle.co.uk
- www.boden.co.uk

Selling your products or services online is the quickest way to start a new business. It's just as easy to broaden your reach if you have an existing bricks-and-mortar business.

> **FOR EXAMPLE:** turn your hobby craft into an online business by selling your glass making, candle products, papercraft or even photography online.

PayPal believe that the relationship between sellers and buyers has always been based on integrity and trust. Trust-building practices, such as personal contact and handshake agreements, are impossible with the internet, but there are ways to communicate honesty and security to your customers while building long-term success.

With your online business, you're likely to be accepting credit and debit card payments and managing names, addresses, phone numbers, email addresses, credit or debit card numbers, and other financial information.

With all this data collection you need to make your customers feel secure by telling them about your business practices, as well as what you plan to do with the personal and financial information they give you. That's what your 'disclosure policy' will detail.

Your responsibility to your customers is to ensure that this personal and financial data is protected. An industry standard known as Payment Card Industry (PCI) Data Security Standard was adopted in 2004 as the result of a collaboration between the various card associations to protect customer information.

As a merchant that stores, processes, and transmits credit card data, you – and your service providers – are required to comply with this payment standard. Like your disclosure policy, your compliance with PCI helps to build good relationships with your customers or clients.

Secure Online Shops

Not too long ago people thought encryption was something only spies did. It brings to mind the world of James Bond and Mission Impossible.

Not anymore! We all undergo encryption without even realising it. Put simply, encryption is a clever piece of technology that allows secure transmission of our data over the internet.

Your customer or client's data entered is encrypted (not visible to anyone, even the user) which means their personal or card details cannot be stolen.

> *"If selling online, it has got to be secure, so partner with the best gateway you can afford to give customers every confidence."*
>
> Polly Gowers, Everyclick

The technology scrambles characters into virtually unreadable gobbledy-gook. You don't need to hold any special keys to decode this babble as it's all done with modern day secure banking.

They use a high level encryption key to automatically encrypt confidential information in transit from your visitor's computer to the bank's servers, which are physically and electronically guarded.

Industry-recognised address Secure Socket Layer (SSL) is a protocol to provide secure communication over the internet. Automated Verification Systems (AVS) and card security code checks thwart identity theft, while patent-pending bank account confirmation adds an additional level of authentication.

Streamlining Transactions

If you intend to sell online you need to work out how you will take care of online payments. There are a multitude of online payment providers all touting their service as the most secure. Their online payment solutions allow you to automate your e-commerce business with all transactions processed directly into your bank account.

"Watch out for charlatans. If a promise sounds too good to be true, it normally is. Do your homework, and don't fall for marketing scams."
Clare Medden, Medden Design

You need to get your website streamlined for transacting with your visitors. You've seen on previous days that most website hosts and designers offer online payment facilities as standard so there should be nothing stopping you.

Merchant Banking

If your business aims to accept payments by credit cards (who doesn't pay this way today?) then you need to set up a merchant account to accept them. Payments will be received directly into your bank account from your merchant account, but this will depend on the deal you make with the merchant bank. Some take their sweet time transferring the money over to you, especially when there are no tangible products involved.

> **FOR EXAMPLE:** if you are selling a service or advertising on your dynamic new site, they will expect to hang on to your money for a week or maybe even longer to ensure there are no returns.

Be careful to check this when calling around. They may say they are flexible, but ask for exact details and get it in writing. Having your money held back by the bank will only impinge on your cash flow and have you chomping at the bit when you need to be buying more goods to feature on your site.

MERCHANT OF THE INTERNET

An Internet Merchant ID can be obtained from any of the UK's acquiring merchant banks, not necessarily your business bank. SecureTrading now offers this as part of their relationships with banks such as Bank of Scotland, Pago, EMS and Elavon.

INTERNATIONAL CURRENCY

Also be sure to ask your Merchant Banker about foreign and international currencies. You don't want to set it all up and then find that they charge way more than the other banker down the street.

GATEWAY TO E-COMMERCE HEAVEN

A gateway, or payment gateway, is how a transaction is processed. When your new customer submits their card details during a transaction this is sent to the bank in real time for authorisation.

While doing your research, consider opening a Business Gateway Account, which will give you everything you need to start collecting online payments. It may be easier to manage with everything under one roof, instead of going round the houses before you see a penny. You can be up and trading in a couple of weeks so check the timings when you make your calls.

Secure Trading

SecureTrading collects and processes credit and debit card payments securely and in real time. They also batch transactions for settlement on a daily basis, provide reports and give merchants the facilities to handle recurring transactions and refunds. This service is also known as a Payment Gateway.

Internet Merchant Ids (MIDs) are obtained from acquiring banks, who need not necessarily be the bank with whom the merchant has a business account.

SecureTrading has relationships with a number of key acquirers and can help merchants obtain these internet MIDs.

Obtaining an Internet MID from an Acquiring Bank is quicker and easier if you already have 'offline' card processing facilities set up with the bank. If merchants have no prior card processing systems the bank will carry out a thorough credit check (lasting anything up to 8 weeks) before authorising them.

PSP: PAYMENT SERVICE PROVIDER

An Internet Payment Service Provider, or PSP, is when online payments are designated as 'cardholder not present' transactions and are considered by acquiring banks as 'higher risk' than 'cardholder present' transactions.

In order to trade online, merchants need to obtain an Internet Merchant ID from the Acquiring bank and also contract with a Payment Service Provider to collect and transmit the card details securely over the Internet. SecureTrading provide solutions in both these areas.

THE PSP MARKET

There are millions of online shoppers spending many more millions each year on the internet. The explosion in online shopping has seen a tightening of online secure payments.

MasterCard SecureCode and Verified by Visa, a credit and debit card authorisation program implemented by Visa and MasterCard, was introduced in 2008 in order to improve consumer confidence and reduce fraud. The technology was made mandatory and millions of cards have been registered.

VIRTUAL TERMINAL

A 'Virtual Terminal' will provide your website with the same functionality as a stand-alone, credit card-processing terminal by enabling you to accept credit card payments by phone, fax, and email.

It also gives you the ability to expand your business off the internet and take payments, even if you don't have a website. PayPal's Virtual Terminal is available either as part of 'Website Payments Pro' or as a standalone solution. For demonstrations of all PayPal's payment solutions and additional information, visit www.paypal-business.co.uk or .com.

Choosing an E-Commerce Partner

They all claim to be the leading suppliers in online secure payments. Don't be fooled by any of that. Do your homework. Have a good ol' Google for 'secure online banking partners' and read everything they have to offer.

176

Then hit the phones and ask some pertinent questions that not only refer to your business and industry, but also to you getting your payments on time.

Some experts would say you can do it all online without even having to pick up the phone, but if you're anything like me, I like to know there is a human on the other end of the phone. So, by giving them a quick buzz you can also be secretly sussing out their customer service.

Ensure you choose an e-commerce partner that can offer you reliability and system availability, as well as great customer service.

In order to operate they must be compliant with Payment Card Industry Data Security Standards (PCI DSS).

The PCI Security Standards Council is an open global forum for the ongoing development, enhancement, storage, dissemination and implementation of security standards for account data protection. Their mission is to enhance payment account data security by driving education and awareness of the PCI Security Standards. The organisation was founded by American Express, Discover Financial Services, JCB International, MasterCard Worldwide and Visa.

Payment Compliance

PayPal advocate that the act of safeguarding your customers' account information communicates how much you care about your customers and reinforces an atmosphere of safety for all online merchants.

Consumers are becoming increasingly aware of the dangers of identity theft due to compromised data and stolen credit card information, so PCI compliance assures your customers that you're looking out for their safety and well-being.

PayPal state that virtually all major credit card companies require merchants and service providers to comply with the PCI standard. When you process credit card transactions through a merchant account, you also need to meet PCI validation requirements, including quarterly and annual audits, security self-assessments, and security scans. Your exact validation requirements are determined the your volume of credit card transactions you process.

The quickest and easiest way to meet PCI compliance standards is to outsource the job. A number of PayPal payment solutions are hosted, relieving the online merchant of the compliance responsibility.

Websites to Research

Check out these websites while you are doing your research; they will be able to help you and answer any further questions you may have.

- www.apacs.org.uk – the UK payments association
- www.cardwatch.org.uk – card fraud awareness organisation
- www.imrg.org – for information about e-retail
- www.getsafeonline.org – safer trading
- www.electronic-payments.co.uk – comparison tool
- www.ecommerce-comparison.com – compares e-commerce providers (not just PSPs)
- www.pcisecuritystandards.org

Questions to Ask

Here is a list of questions to keep in mind when making your calls.

IMPORTANT QUESTIONS

- ❑ Do they take foreign currency payments?
- ❑ Do you need a merchant banking account?
- ❑ Do they have a gateway all in one system?
- ❑ What are their standard monthly charges?
- ❑ What are their card charges for credit cards versus debit cards?
- ❑ How long will it take for transaction funds to be transferred into your account?
- ❑ Are there any other charges you need to know about?
- ❑ What timelines you should be aware of?

Data Protection

The Data Protection Act gives your customers the right to know what information is held about them, and sets out rules to make sure that you handle this information properly. PayPal advises that clear, concise details on your Data Protection practices will reinforce your customer relationships and foster an environment of trust. It is also a legal requirement as all organisations must make sure that they comply with the Data Protection Act.

HOW THE DATA PROTECTION ACT WORKS

As I say, it gives your customers the right to know what information is held about them, and sets out rules to make sure that this information is handled properly. Should an individual or organisation feel they're being denied access to personal information they're entitled to, or feel their information has not been handled accordingly, they can contact the Information Commissioner's Office for help. Complaints are usually dealt with informally, but if this isn't possible, enforcement action can be taken.

It requires all organisations which handle personal information to comply with eight important principles regarding privacy and disclosure.

Anyone who processes personal information must make sure that their customer's personal information is:

- Secure
- Fairly and lawfully processed
- Processed for limited purposes
- Adequate, relevant and not excessive
- Accurate and up to date
- Not kept for longer than is necessary
- Processed in line with your rights
- Not transferred to other countries without adequate protection

GET MORE INFORMATION

- DPA: Data Protection Act 1998
- ECD: Electronic Commerce Regulations 2002 (EC Directive)

Easy Ways To Sell Online

In saying all of the above, there are also easier ways to start selling immediately. Having a Merchant ID is ideal if you are serious about making money on a long term basis and is pretty much dependant on your site's needs.

However, you can set up a PayPal or Google Checkout Account and be trading in minutes rather than waiting days or weeks for merchant applications to go through. As I said at the beginning of today's chapter, they all charge a fee for the transaction so compare the percentages and decide for yourself.

When you set up an account in PayPal and Google Checkout, trial them both for separate products or services and see which is best. You will need to verify your account so they know it's really you.

> *"Traffic! Who wants to live on a busy road?*
> *Interested customers are what you want. Target*
> *those, not just hit rates and traffic noise."*
> Clare Medden, Medden Design

They simply deposit a tiny amount in pennies into your account and send you an email to remind you to verify the account. Once you've checked your bank statement, you go online to verify the exact amounts and your account is activated.

PayPal's service called 'Website Payments Standard' is a fast, simple way to start selling online. You just add a payment button to your site and you'll be able to accept payments from all major credit and debit cards, as well as bank accounts around the world. There are no upfront costs, no set-up or monthly fees and there's no financial outlay to worry about. Best of all, you don't need any advanced technical knowledge; it's just a button to copy and paste.

Their 'Website Payments Pro' is an all-in-one payment solution that allows your customers to shop and make payments on your website without redirection to PayPal pages. You can accept credit cards directly on your site, or through a virtual terminal, and get the features of a merchant account and gateway through a single provider at a lower cost. Website Payments Pro allows you to control your checkout from start to finish.

LINKS
- www.checkout.google.com
- www.paypal.com or www.paypal.co.uk
- www.1shoppingcart.com
- www.securetrading.com

GADGETS AND WIDGETS

Most of the providers offer widgets and gadgets to show off your secure trading symbols. Use them to gain your visitors' trust so they'll be happy to spend their money with you.

DELIVERY

You've made the sale. Your customers are anxious to get their purchases, so keep that excitement and positive momentum going with a delivery policy that's simple and straightforward.

PayPal advises that you spell out your delivery terms in detail, disclosing if costs are determined by weight or the amount of the purchase. You should also indicate the types of delivery you offer - ground, express or overnight, as well as where you deliver to, or do not deliver. Your customers also need to know when to expect their purchase and if they can track their shipment.

REFUNDS

It's extra work for you to juggle, but people make mistakes and order the wrong products. They may be unfamiliar with what they are ordering or the product they receive is not what they had in mind. Either way, you should allow your customers to return or cancel an item.

This way you will gain loyalty and trust from them and they will more than likely return. Remember that sticky stuff we crawled over yesterday? This is another way to get tacky with your visitors.

A clear return and refund policy also comes in handy if the order arrives damaged. So make it easy for them to initiate returns. PayPal suggests you spell out your exact return policy.

PAYPAL'S RETURN POLICY EXAMPLE
- Accept returns only as exchanges
- Accept returns and credit their payment card
- Be specific about how many days after purchase the item can be returned in order to get a refund or exchange
- Let them know if you charge a restocking fee on returns
- Include a return shipping label with every order
- Include your customer service number or email address in case customers have questions or comments
- Provide clear return instructions, such as asking for a reason for the return and a telephone number in case you have questions
- In the event that an order is cancelled make sure you specify clear terms and conditions

Last Word

As with all areas of your website or internet business, you should feature open channels of communication to make it easy for your visitors to get in touch with you.

If they have purchased an item from your site, there are often questions to ask and they need to get in contact with you by phone or email. As I have said before, make this information visible and show it in numerous places to ensure their trust. After all, you do want them to return again and again and ... you get the picture!

You should set up a disclosure policy, which will show your customers that you're honest and dependable and most importantly, that you care about protecting their information and that you believe in transparency and accountability.

PayPal advises that your disclosure policy should include five things: a business description, privacy policy, delivery policy, refund and cancellation policy and your contact information. The more your customers know about you, the more they'll feel good about giving you their business. So be honest, open, direct, and precise.

Summary

As an online shop it is vital you get set up with a first class e-commerce solution and so today we talked about the various options to choose and their pros and cons.

We realised that the most important step is to interact with your audience and to do this safely with all the mod-cons out in the online market place. Merchant banking, encryption and gateways were all part of our focus. We also discussed some quick and easy ways to start selling online.

We chatted briefly about a refunds and disclosure policy to ensure your customers feel protected so they will trust you and your online business.

Now that you are ready for your customers and able to catch them in your e-commerce net, we will move on to find ways to earn an income from your site.

Checklist

- ❏ Keep your list of questions handy
- ❏ Secure online banking
- ❏ Merchant Banker
- ❏ Gateway Partner
- ❏ PayPal
- ❏ Google Checkout

Day 9: Revenue

Catch 'Em While You Can

Be ready for impulse buyers. In the world of fast speed internet, you need to maintain a buyer's momentum if they have an instinctive urge to trade with your site. Gone are the days when you could give out a number and expect someone to ring you.

The phone may never ring, but your shopping trolley could be spinning its wheels with sales. If someone sees a product on your site at 3am when they can't sleep, they expect to buy it immediately. Be ready for them and catch them in your e-commerce net.

Most of the software and instant sites we talked about earlier have easy integration with PayPal or Google Checkout. So, today we'll examine a variety of ways to earn an income from your website.

KAREN HANTON FROM TOPTABLE ADVISES...

- Online advertising really is developing fast - providing you can prove the quality and quantity of your audience.

- Always get a third party survey of who your users are as brand managers need to justify spending their dollars with you.

The most obvious way is to sell products or services, but there are lots of other ways to earn an income. Having multiple revenue streams will strengthen your business while you build your customer base.

FOR EXAMPLE: you may bake fancy occasional cakes, craft beautiful wedding cakes or create specialist icing designs as a hobby. A website will show off your creations to a larger local or regional audience and earn an income from your passion. You can even create an e-book sharing some of your tips for baking and cake decorating enthusiasts.

The most important step is to interact with your audience.

Also bear in mind that your site might be a hobby site or a student portfolio site to begin with, but it could soon turn into a revenue generating website.

> **FOR EXAMPLE:** as a student or graduate you may set up a portfolio of your work at University. You may even earn a small income as a freelancer for local and regional companies or selling goods to other students, which could eventually become a fully fledged online business.

Monetise Your Site

This section will help to identify new opportunities. Depending on the type of site, your theme, targeted visitors and site audience, your product or service offering, there may be a variety of ways to earn an income. These could include:

- Affiliate Marketing
- E-books, e-News or articles
- Membership programs or subscriptions
- Google Adsense
- Banner advertising and online display adverts
- Amazon aStore (see earlier chapter)
- Lead generation
- Sponsorships and partnerships
- Tutorials and podcasts

We'll go through these topics in this chapter.

 AFFILIATE MARKETING

- **Selling products through a commission scheme.**
- **Selling from an Advertiser's point of view.**
- **Earning revenue from an Affiliate's point of view.**

Affiliate Marketing

Sanjit Atwal, UK Head of Publisher Services & Development of TradeDoubler defines Affiliate Marketing as a working relationship whereby a merchant (an online shop, merchant or advertiser) has consumers driven to it by adverts on an affiliate website.

If a consumer visiting the affiliate's site clicks on an advertisement and goes on to perform a predetermined action, usually a purchase on the advertiser's site, then the affiliate (possibly your website), receives a payment. This predetermined action can range from a sale to a referral, a newsletter sign-up to a click. It is this 'cost per action' model that defines affiliate marketing and sets it apart from other channels.

IN A NUTSHELL

For the advertiser: affiliate marketing is all about selling products on a commission basis.

For the affiliate: affiliate marketing is all about earning commission from adverts on your site that produce sales.

Affiliate marketing works two ways:

ADVERTISER OR MERCHANT: This is when you are either the merchant (an offline or online shop) or advertiser and you ask affiliates or publishers to drive sales of your products in exchange for a financial reward.

AFFILIATE OR PUBLISHER: This is where you're the affiliate, also known as a website publisher, and you drive traffic to someone else's website, usually the advertiser or merchant, on the agreement that any sales resulting from this action earns you a commission.

Some websites can be both and you can earn revenue as both an affiliate and an advertiser, so first let's take a look from an affiliate's perspective, then we'll discuss how to become an advertiser to sell your products through other affiliates.

Affiliate or Publisher

Affiliate marketing is performance-based online marketing. You promote somebody else's products on your website in exchange for a commission. When a person browsing your site buys a product after following the link you displayed, you earn a commission for the sale.

SANJIT ATWAL FROM TRADEDOUBLER BELIEVES...

- Affiliates are virtual sales teams
- Affiliate marketing is all about 'cost per action'

Remember we discussed setting up an Amazon aStore? Being an affiliate marketer is similar; the only difference is that Amazon gives you the ability to set up a whole affiliate shop, whereas affiliate networks will arm you with all the marketing materials, such as graphic adverts, to sell other products.

Affiliate programmes can generate revenue from and for your site, but before you get affiliate-happy, be aware that to be successful, and earn a good income, you will need high traffic figures and relevant content.

"Don't expect to make your fortune from affiliate marketing unless you have significant traffic."
Carrie Longton, Mumsnet

Affiliate programmes give you access to online merchants who will pay you a commission for generating sales, leads, or applications. How much you earn depends on the products you choose to promote and how relevant they are to your site's content. Ultimately, the biggest keys to success are traffic and conversion. You need an audience of potential online shoppers to talk to, and you then need to place relevant ads in front of them to ensure they are converting from prospects to buyers.

Pros:
- ✓ No set up fees for web publishers to open an affiliate account
- ✓ Free to join merchant programmes, although some will set restrictions for certain types of web publishers
- ✓ Merchants will provide graphic banners and tracking for you to use on your site
- ✓ Huge variety of products and services available to promote
- ✓ No merchant banking needed
- ✓ Shop always open
- ✓ Potential high income if you have a high level of targeted traffic
- ✓ Requires few resources
- ✓ New technologies provide quick and easy ways to get and share links

Cons:

- ✗ Need high traffic to generate enough income
- ✗ Can clutter your website with ads and ruin your brand
- ✗ Beware of lowering your brand value with inappropriate ads

Choose to promote merchants or products that will appeal to your audience and once you've established a track record, see if you can increase the commission you receive per sale.

> *"Seek out merchants and strike your own deals!"*
> Carrie Longton, Mumsnet

Affiliates typically earn a percentage of the sale when they send a user to a merchant's website and they make a purchase. Merchants usually look after their affiliates (their virtual sales team) by providing plenty of banners, text links, product feeds and discount codes. You need to use a company that specialises in affiliate marketing such as affiliate networks. They set you up with the tools to track the sales you generate, the commissions you are due and provide a place to access merchant's banners and product feeds.

HOW IT WORKS

Each time one of your visitors clicks an advert on your site and then makes a purchase from that advert, you earn a commission. Therefore the term 'earnings per click' means: commission ÷ clicks = EPC.

Sanjit recommends that you consider:

- Advertiser Relevance – ads must be suited to your target audience
- Creative – which banners would suit your site?
- Commercials – specific to your visitor requirements
- Tracking and Reporting – must be easy and accessible

Here's how seamless the affiliate purchase process is:

1. User browses affiliate site and clicks on an advert
2. Clicks are tracked through an invisible re-direct page
3. The Affiliate Network drops a cookie identifying the affiliate before user is sent to the merchant site
4. User browses merchant site and selects a product to purchase

189

5. Sale is recorded and commission awarded to affiliate

WHAT TO LOOK FOR

Depending on your individual needs, Jacqueline Cox from Affiliate Window advises affiliates to work with merchant programmes that can prove higher conversion rates, higher EPC and shorter validation periods where possible. The most important advice is to choose merchants that are a good fit for your own website.

> **FOR EXAMPLE:** if you are a fashion site work with fashion merchants. Promote merchants or products that are relevant to your audience.

Jacky suggests that you need to research the programmes yourself, but Affiliate Window also provides lots of useful statistics through your affiliate account that enables you to do this. If you need details on how Affiliate Window's tracking works and to see a range of their merchants, banners and links, Jacky suggests you read their Wiki at http://wiki.affiliatewindow.com

Some factors to think about:

- What is the general potential to earn money i.e. what commission is the merchant offering and how well does their site convert traffic?
- Does the merchant have a PPC (Pay Per Click) policy?
- How quickly do they approve and pay commissions?
- Many networks will have minimum earning levels before paying out your commission; therefore you only get paid once you have reached a certain level. For example, they may set the minimum level at £100 and it may take ages before you earn while your traffic builds.
- Check the network's terms and conditions for any hidden charges

HOW TO JOIN AN AFFILIATE NETWORK

As an affiliate (or publisher) most networks are free to join, and the sign-up process is generally very simple. Once you have joined the network, you must apply to each of the merchant programmes that you want to join.

"Affiliate Marketing forms the 'action'
in the marketing mix."
Sanjit Atwal, TradeDoubler

If you're after fashion houses you will have to apply to each individual brand within the affiliate network. Some may accept you straight away, while others need to manually vet your application. Others may even decline your application if they feel your site is not a good fit with theirs, or if your site is 'too young' and requires further development. Most networks will have a sign up form to fill out on their website, which will ask a few basic questions about your website or promotional methods. Generally, applications are approved within 24-48 hours.

WHICH AFFILIATE NETWORKS

If you want unbiased advice about networks from individuals working within the industry, you can find this on the Affiliates4U forum at www.affiliates4u.com.

As an affiliate you benefit from a single point of contact to handle commissions from multiple merchants. The network tracks your commission and analyses activity. Networks also represent the interests of affiliates, ensuring that merchants provide good quality creative adverts and that a support team is in place to answer any questions.

There are a variety of networks to choose from and each has its own strengths. Make sure to look at the choice of programmes on each network and select the one (or ones) with the right products relevant to your site.

WHAT NEXT?

Once your account is up and running, you choose the banners, text links, videos or product images to display on your site. Most linking methods are available in multiple sizes. All you do is copy and paste the code into your website and, like magic, it appears on your page.

Any sales, and the corresponding commissions, that are generated from these links are then tracked within your network account. Keep in mind that you may choose to work with multiple networks and therefore you will not be able to see your total earnings through one account; you will need to log-in separately to each network.

> *"The Internet Advertising Bureau ensures that traffic from affiliate sites sent to merchants is not done in a misleading or confusing way so that consumers receive a good user experience."*
> Sanjit Atwal, TradeDoubler

AFFILIATE NETWORKS TO TRY

Please look into each carefully before signing up. Joining the right one is dependent on the relevancy of the merchants it represents in relation to your site users. If you have a site that reviews the latest gadgets then you will want to join all of the networks that allow you to get links for brands such as Firebox.com, Play.com and Prezzybox. Alternatively, if you have a Harry Potter fan-site then you would want to work with any merchant who sells the books, films or merchandise including HMV, WH Smiths and Toys R Us.

- TradeDoubler: www.tradedoubler.com
- Affiliate Future: www.affiliatefuture.com
- Affiliate Window: www.affiliatewindow.com
- Affilinet: www.affili.net
- Buy.at: www.buy.at
- Commission Junction: www.cj.com
- Dgm: www.dgm-uk.com
- LinkShare: www.linkshare.co.uk
- MoreNiche: www.moreniche.com
- OMG: www.omgpm.com
- Paid on Results: www.paidonresults.com
- TradeDoubler: www.tradedoubler.com
- Webgains: www.webgains.com

 ALSO CHECK OUT...
...the Internet Advertising Bureau – www.iabuk.net

KEEPING TRACK OF EARNINGS

Keep track of merchant commissions so you can figure out which ones are worth maintaining. Use these headings in a simple spreadsheet:

- ❏ Name of Merchant
- ❏ URL
- ❏ Number of Clicks
- ❏ Number of Sales Generated
- ❏ Total Value of Sales Generated
- ❏ Total Commissions Earned
- ❏ Conversion Rate
- ❏ Average Earnings Per Sale

Your affiliate network should provide flexible, easy-to-read reports that can help you to analyse your activity and help you drive results.

Alternatively, you can use a software provider such as Staagg (www.staagg.com), which will aggregate all of your statistics from across the different networks, giving you an instant overview of your daily performance through their intuitive affiliate reporting suite.

QUESTIONS FOR AFFILIATES TO ASK

- ❏ Are you allowed to use trademarks in your Ad copy title?
- ❏ Are you allowed to use trademarks in your Ad copy body?
- ❏ Are you allowed to show adverts on misspellings of advertiser's trademarks?
- ❏ Are you allowed to show adverts for a search on advertiser's Company Name and trademarks?
- ❏ Are you allowed to show adverts for a search on advertiser's Company Name or trademarks when also using generic terms?
- ❏ Are you allowed to show adverts against advertiser's URL (e.g. www.emerchant.com)?
- ❏ Are you allowed to show adverts against advertiser's URL or variations of it?
- ❏ Are you allowed to show adverts on trademarks, or variations, of advertiser's competitors?
- ❏ Are you allowed to show adverts for generic terms when using a landing page?

❑ Negative keywords list/Trademarks - are you dis-allowed from showing adverts for a straight search on any trademarked or excluded terms (eg 'waterstones', 'waterstone's')?

Advertiser or Merchant

As I mentioned earlier, this is another way to earn revenue through affiliate marketing. As an advertiser you will be showing off your products on other people's websites and when someone clicks on the advert you supply them, you pay them commission for every sale.

Being an advertiser on an affiliate network gives small businesses a definite return on investment. If you think about advertising as branding and association with a lifestyle (if there is no special offer message), think about affiliate marketing as converting traffic from other sites to sales and paying that site a commission for their help. Therefore it offers a direct return and real incentive for the affiliate to promote your business, rather than general advertising which could deliver interest, attention and desire, but not necessarily immediate action.

Sounds easy, doesn't it?

It can be if you have the resources and infrastructure to implement an advertiser or merchant programme. Remember Sanjit referred to affiliates as virtual sales teams, so if you want to reach a new sales force and attract them to your cause then a 'cost per action' model in your business may be an option for you.

Pros:

✓ Getting bigger every month
✓ Quick turn around
✓ Creative sales solutions
✓ Extended sales force (virtually via other sites)
✓ Return on investment model
✓ Opportunities in mobile commerce, iPad, Apps

Cons:

✗ Requires resource
✗ May have costly set up charges
✗ Product knowledge is key
✗ Competitive market

- ✗ Requires tech changes on advertiser site
- ✗ Can be confusing to newcomers
- ✗ Susceptible to consumer behaviour

Sanjit advises new advertisers to consider the following before making a final decision:

- ❑ What do I want to sell?
- ❑ Are all of the products I want to sell on the same domain?
- ❑ How are the products grouped by category?
- ❑ What are my margins by category?
- ❑ What is the maximum I can afford to pay for one sale by category?

KEYWORD POLICY

- ❑ Can you include trademarks in the sub folders of the display URL's in your Search Engine Adverts? For example: www.AffiliateSite.com/AdvertiserName
- ❑ Can you include trademarks in the sub domain of the display URL's in your Search Engine Adverts? For example: www.AdvertiserName.AffiliateSite.com
- ❑ Can you operate domains which contain trademarks for the sole purpose of driving traffic from Search Engines? For example: www.AdvertiserName.com

In summary, there is much to examine for both a publisher and merchant account and it is not to be taken lightly. Read extensively, learn from the experts and ask as many questions as it takes before you embark into Affiliate Marketing.

E-News

A regular e-newsletter is an excellent way to show off your great 'sticky' content and to kick start a 'working' relationship with your visitors.

Some company e-newsletters exist solely to generate huge profits and if you want to do this, think back to your long term plans as it could take some time to get to this level. Think big!

The more targeted and niche your audience, the more in demand your list will be and it could, one day, become a big income driver. For now, add this to your revenue streams and when you've built up a large database you will be more aware of how to make this happen and ensure success. I have a whole chapter on email marketing in *Pimp My Site* so I hope you will continue on your journey with me and read my next book.

Lead Generation

A good way to generate leads could be to partner with other sites that are relevant, yet not competitors. Look around for potential partners and ask them for a link exchange as a starter.

Once you have shown trust by giving them the link and any other ideas they requested, ask if they want to work with you on promotions and lead generation.

Consider what you can do in return for them giving you a helping hand. You can also offer them a fee for every item bought from their site. You will need to implement a 'How Heard', which can be simple enough if added to a PayPal button or your web developer can add this in as hard coded HTML. Only pay for signed up or paid for leads. A transaction must take place or you'll be paying through your nose for nothing.

> *"Swap links with anyone who has like-minded users.*
> *Make sure your site is SEO friendly and useful!"*
> Carrie Longton, Mumsnet

There are cost effective ways to get started and Jon Buxton suggests, if you're in the nursery industry, you might talk to the NCT or place inserts into bounty packs that parents receive when they have a baby. See if there is a trade show or exhibition associated with your market and see what opportunities are available.

JON BUXTON ON COMPETITIONS...
Competitions are a great way to generate lists of names, email addresses etc. People won't mind submitting their details to you if there is the possibility of winning a lovely prize. You can then use this information in future mail shots. For the people that don't win you can mail them and offer them a discount code.

Subscriptions

Another form of monetising a site and achieve a steady stream of income is by selling memberships or subscriptions. You could start by giving free memberships to build a user base and then offer varying subscription levels.

While membership sites offer many advantages, there is lots of content filling involved as well as interaction with the members. Above all, if you want to get constant sign ups you need to provide value for money. There are so many of these around today so you have to have a unique offering for memberships that your visitors will want and need. Think long and hard about your expertise, your training, your product or service and then do a brainstorming session to find lots of lateral streams for possible membership packages.

You may also want to collaborate with other sites or partners to come up with a subscription stuffed full with helpful products or services, important resources and content or access areas. And it needs to be a place they want to return to again and again.

The more you give your members and the more you stay in touch, the greater your chances of building customer loyalty and thus urging them to tell others about your membership. You can even offer them an incentive or special offer for spreading the word.

Consider adding an opt-in mailing list, an advertising list, directory or promotional list, which gives you an added stream for earning revenue. Maybe you can offer your paying members a way to advertise their products or services through your site.

With this in mind, you may even want to create a niche 'Online Directory'. This will be dependent on your site's content, theme and traffic. It's a long term strategy rather than a quick money return as it will take time and elbow grease to build and to gain search engine placements. Think about offering this free to start with and then charge for listings later on when it has proven to be successful. Or you can offer a free trial. However, you will need to give them a long term deal until you are sure they are receiving traffic, leads or conversions. Otherwise why will they want to pay for it?

Online Advertising

The past few years have proved to be an extremely exciting time for online advertising. So much is changing so quickly, we have to be on our tippy-toes to keep up. Companies, both large and small, are spending more money on online advertising than any other media. The more niche your audience the more likely your site will be in demand.

First though, decide what is best for your business. In other words, you can't do it all so prioritise and evaluate selling online advertising against your goals and targets for your online business.

Advertising sales is the main source of income for Mumsnet, but Carrie believes you need lots of traffic to make this work.

When advertising is targeted, it can be a good revenue earner as in the case of Babyworld, which is specific to pregnant women and parents with children up to 5 years. However, having adverts from 'just anyone' could be negative and Debbie is careful in selecting relevant advertisers for the site.

ADVERTISING TIPS

Debbie says:
- ✓ Have a clear idea of who and what would work well advertising on your site
- ✓ Ensure a clear strategy for your advertisers

Polly says:
- ✓ Don't waste your time trying to sell advertising
- ✓ Use the best advertising programmes out there, such as Google Adwords

Banners

There are various forms of online advertising and Banner Advertising is one of them. This can also be done through the Affiliate Marketing we discussed earlier or directly through advertisers and media buying agencies.

Think about great TV and newspaper ads; what attracted you to them and why? Do analysis on your competitors' sites and other relevant sites to see which advertisers are featured.

Make notes of these or, better still, contact them straight away if your site is ready to show off to prospective advertisers. Remember that the advertiser's goal for their banner ad is to raise awareness for their brand as well as drive traffic to their site, so they will have created their message with a particular target audience in mind.

If that ideal audience is yours, their ad will do well on your site. Give the advertiser value for money by extending the time the banner is featured on your site, especially if you are still new with small traffic figures. That way, as your traffic grows, hopefully so will their response.

"When Mumsnet started we swapped banners,
now they are a source of income and we have a
sales team to sell them."
Carrie Longton, Mumsnet

Of course you value their business and want them to keep advertising with you, so give them extra bonuses by featuring their ad on different pages to see the best results. Do whatever you can to retain your advertising clients because they may become your bread and butter clients in future.

The success of a banner ad depends largely on the message contained within it. It doesn't need to be flashy or brightly coloured, instead, Jon advocates that readers need to see something that will persuade them to click on it. This can be a discount code or the possibility to win a prize.

Focus your banners towards the audience that you are targeting. Banner swaps with other companies give you an opportunity to get your message to a wider audience without spending a lot of money on advertising. However, make sure that you can measure the number of times your banner is served and the click through rate of the banner. There are simple and cost effective banner management software programmes available that you can incorporate into your website.

Polly Gowers from Everyclick advises: Don't expect miracles. You should focus your energies on talking to real users.

WHICH BANNERS TO CHOOSE
Don't clutter your site with banners and do be careful to choose adverts that compliment your brand. Busy, loud and awful clipart banners can wipe out all your 'branding' hard work in a flash.

Complex flashy banners also slow down your page load rate so your visitors may just bounce away if your page is too slow to upload because of your advertising banners.

Don't be desperate to take someone's money. If there's a chance of lowering your standards By accepting an advertiser then don't do it. It's not worth it! Instead, find companies that use good images and focus on a clear message that will appeal to your visitors.

Like affiliate links, banner advertising has little impact unless you have high footfall going through your site. You can put your toe in the water gently by testing out a few banners from Google's Adsense programme.

Google Adsense
Online ad giant, Google, offers you a way to get advertising content onto your site and earn money. You'll get paid for displaying targeted ads on your site from the large pool of Google advertisers using their service. This way you don't have to go out and look for them and a lot of the hard work on making the ads relevant is done for you.

Some online entrepreneurs claim to have made big money this way, but again this could have been due to high traffic figures.

HERE'S HOW IT WORKS
1. Choose where to show your ads. Specify where you want the ads to appear and choose the type of adverts you want.
2. Advertisers bid in a real-time auction and you get to always show the highest paying adverts.

3. Google bills their advertising network and you get paid for your contribution.

4. Choose relevant ads to suit your page content and the format that they are displayed.

5. Adverts can be targeted according to demographics, vertical markets and geographic locations.

6. Be sure to protect your brand by limiting certain sites and avoiding spam-ertisers. You can block certain URLs or categories. For example, if you are a family site, block adult and gambling adverts.

7. Your reports will help you to monitor how your Adsense income was earned, by specific day or date, by page and areas and by clicks or impressions.

Sponsorship Success

The Remote Worker Awards is a great sponsorship initiative. One of the ways we decided to increase our traffic levels and raise awareness for remote and home workers was to honour individuals and companies who champion this way of working.

So we set about to find an ideal headline sponsor and we approached BT Business. We also used the opportunity to ensure we had the most unique awards in the country by offering valuable prizes.

I was talking to one company about sponsoring the home based franchise section of Remote Employment and suddenly I had a light bulb moment and blurted out that they could sponsor a home based franchise for the Awards.

CARRIE LONGTON FROM MUMSNET ON PARTNERSHIPS...

- **Start by identifying sites with a similar user base and values.**
- **Swap inventory and page impressions. It makes your site look busy and brings you 'eyeballs'.**

I immediately realised my 'blunder' as a prize of that kind had a £15,000 value. However, they thought it was a great idea and The Helen O' Grady Special Award became our flagship award. It was extremely exciting and highly rewarding to know we would change someone's life overnight by giving them this substantial prize.

We also approached other companies to sponsor Award Categories to get their business associated with other top brands, such as BT, and they would get the constant PR attention the Awards generated. £75,000 in prizes is not bad for a first timer in the awards arena!

The inaugural Awards press releases were circulated to 145 million readers and we achieved almost a million pounds in positive PR coverage. We were staggered with the results, but proved to ourselves that this is not only the most unique award in the country, but we also helped to change lives by giving people their own home based business.

In our second year we decided to get each award category sponsored by a high profile brand and we ended up working with Microsoft, Lexmark and Blackberry along with BT. We also gained even more media attention and we were featured on ITV Meridian three times! Check out the awards news coverage page to see the PR we achieved.

SPONSORS

If you have a niche site with a specialist audience, as we have with Remote Employment and The Remote Worker Awards you may find that asking certain clients to sponsor areas of your site or individual pages is better than banner advertising.

Brainstorm or iMindMap some ideas for potential sponsorship partners and always keep your eyes peeled for new opportunities.

SPONSORSHIP PRESENTATIONS

There is more to ask for than just money. Don't get me wrong, money is the cherry on the top, but you will benefit by working with big brands so think about what they could do for your business. As well as gaining credibility it could provide another advantage. It also gives you the chance to 'name drop' and if you get a great brand on board, tell other potential sponsors who'll all clamber to be associated.

Sponsorships are not just about monetary value and bringing credibility to your brand, they also give your audience a kinship with the sponsor. You should also come up with ways that you can help the sponsor and things you can do for them in return. If the sponsor is paying you, they will want to see marketing and publicity value for their sponsorship. We showed our sponsors for The Remote Worker Awards excellent value by pumping out PR and gaining high media coverage for all of them.

SPONSORSHIP IDEAS

- Book launch
- Product launch
- Research – new or existing products
- Events
- Awards
- Product placement
- Book or product tour

FORMS OF SPONSORSHIP

- Cash sponsorship in return for something from you
- Product placement – they place products on your site and you possibly do the same in return
- Email their clients about your product or service and you do the same for them
- Case studies of your offering can be shared amongst their network or members
- Ask to be featured on their website
- Provide free tickets to your event in return for being featured on their website, in their magazine or newsletters

HOW TO APPROACH A SPONSOR

Research the companies you choose and approach their Press Officer or Media Centre Spokesperson. Most sites show this on their news or press page. The Press Officer may handle sponsorships but if not they can probably put you in touch with the marketing department or their Media Agency.

A personal approach is always best so you can show them your enthusiasm and passion for your subject and project. Once you have identified a list of possible sponsors, call them and ask them if you can take a few moments of their time. Be ready with your proposal and what's the benefit to them. Don't go into all the specifics on the phone, rather give them a brief outline and then forward the details by email or ask for a face-to-face meeting.

They may only want to deal with you via email, but do ask for a meeting and, if they agree, go to their offices prepared to do a presentation.

As I mentioned in the early pages of the book under 'who should read this book', if you are an 'up-and-coming' sports personality, sponsorships will be easier to secure if you have a sparkling website.

> **FOR EXAMPLE:** you will need to have different pages for your achievements and skills. Don't be shy to ask openly for sponsors to approach you – if you don't ask who will? Remember to highlight the benefits of working with you to entice a sponsor to make contact.

Partnerships

For the second Remote Worker Awards, we decided to work with various Media Partners. After the success of the first year, we were thrilled to get some fantastic partners on board for the second year.

Business Matters, Babyworld, Strategic HR Review, Berkshire and Buckinghamshire Life, What Franchise and Making Money all jumped on board. They promoted the Awards to their readers. We gave them pages on the Awards site in return and their benefit was the association with our 'big name' sponsors, including BT Business.

THE MORAL OF THE STORY: Cherry pick your partners, decide what you want to do and how it will work and the benefits to your partner. Do thorough in-depth home work, then, approach them with a sure-fire proposal.

BABYWORLD'S JON BUXTON ON PARTNERSHIPS...

- **Some partnerships work and some don't.**
- **Manage these alliances carefully and make sure that there is mutual benefit to both parties.**
- **Sometimes charities are in a position to work with commercial partners – they may provide you with valuable publicity. Support them by providing links, competition prizes or expert advice on a given subject.**

Tutorials and Podcasts

We've talked about selling products, but what about trainers and service providers? You can earn revenue for your site with podcasts, video workshops and tutorials. You have all the skill, knowledge and expertise, now all you have to do it implement some crafty ways of delivering it and selling it online. You can either sell workshops and training master classes, as I do through my personal website (www.paulawynne.com/workshops.html). Create a video tutorial or podcast and allow people to learn from you online. I too will be setting up some of these as many people who are far flung across the country have requested online training. Take a look at other services to see how they deliver their tutorials and then follow the best examples.

Wow KPIs

What on earth is a KPI? A Key Performance Indicator, or KPI, identifies and quantifies key areas of your website as the best or worst performers.

If you are planning to have an investor or Non Executive Director on board as mentioned earlier in the book, they will want to see your KPIs at your monthly meetings.

The KPIs will give you a good idea of how your online business is growing, what areas are weak and which are strongest. This information will show you what opportunities lie ahead. If done in neat little graphs, they will quickly and clearly show you how well your site is performing and where to focus your energy. Try setting up graphs in Excel early on to monitor your traffic, your products, different services, your revenue and any other important indicators of success.

> **FOR EXAMPLE:** in Remote Employment we track and monitor our jobs through KPIs as well as our traffic growth.

After the first year of The Remote Worker Awards, we set up KPIs to reflect the PR we generated, the circulation we covered, the media response and, of course, the number of yearly applications. It is great fun and highly satisfying when you see the graph on a steep upward climb! If you have a large range of products then try it out and clearly see your bestsellers.

THE MORAL OF THE STORY: Clever stats will WOW your visitors, partners, sponsors, management board, bank manager and anyone else who happens to be interested. Be proud to show off your growth, whilst keeping key information confidential. It is important that as much of this information as possible is visible to the business media as well.

Summary

Even though the most obvious way to earn revenue from a website is to sell products or a service, we have found that there are lots of other ways to earn an income. Having multiple revenue streams will strengthen your business while you build your customer base. Do this by finding different ways to generate money and use lateral thinking for creative ways to promote your products or service.

Today, we also took the opportunity to explore affiliates, banner advertising, lead generation, sponsorships and Google Adsense - all good ways to create steady profits.

Checklist

- ❑ Revenue Ideas
- ❑ Affiliate marketing?
- ❑ Research different affiliate programmes
- ❑ Affiliate spreadsheet
- ❑ Banner ads or banner swap
- ❑ Lead generation
- ❑ Try Google Adsense
- ❑ Approach potential sponsors
- ❑ Build partnerships
- ❑ Establish KPIs

Day 10: Go Live

Open for Business

Today we talk about 'Going Live' and all that you need to do to prepare and be ready for the big day.

I would recommend that you start to publicise and market your site by what is known as 'drip feeding', which simply means lots of little bits, like a leaking tap. So, I have chosen to end the book on a high note with the going live process. Your PR and marketing campaign starts full time after you have gone live and that process never ends.

We'll chat about the steps to take before you go live, setting up and using your Google Analytics account and adding your site to your Google account. We will also go over your final checklist and how to fill your site so that it looks good, fat and full before you show it off to the world.

Go live is a very exciting time, but it is also a huge 'time-hoover' and you need to be on your toes to ensure everything gets done and all your tests are completed before you hit the big green button.

Steps Before Go Live

Google Analytics is the easiest way for you to track your traffic and analyse your website statistics. Once you have opened your Google Analytics account, it will give you code to copy and paste into your home page. This is so they can verify that you own the site before you start tracking the traffic.

Tracking Traffic With Google

Once your site is up and running you need to add your site to Google to track your traffic. Here is a step-by-step guide to adding tracking code to your website:

CREATE NEW WEBSITE PROFILE

Follow these steps to set up a new profile in Google Analytics:

1. In your Google Account, at the top is 'account settings', click this.
2. It will open 'My Products' - hit the 'Analytics' link.
3. You will now see an 'overview' of your Analytics account, where you can add a number of sites and blogs. At the bottom is an 'Add Website Profile' link.
4. Another page called 'Create New Website Profile' opens where you can add a profile for a new domain.
5. Also, add your domain and territory.

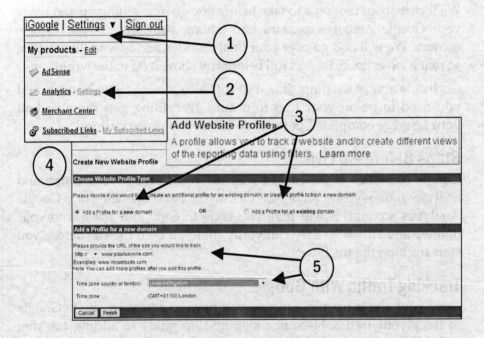

ADD TRACKING CODE

Follow these steps to add a tracking code to your Google Analytics account:

6. You will now see your domain name in the 'overview' page, so click the 'Edit' link on the far right.

7. A profile page will open which will probably state in the corner above the box 'Tracking not installed (Check Status)' – this is the link to click.

8. Copy and paste the code into your page, immediately before the </body> tag of each page you are planning to track.

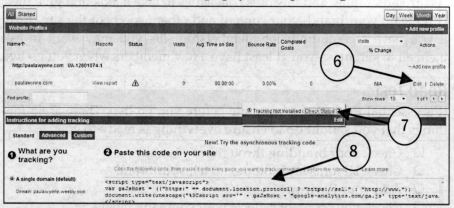

Hosted and pay monthly sites should include this service, so add this to your question checklist to ensure you get some help with it.

WEBSITE PROVIDER

Adding tracking could be easier and it depends on your website provider. In the Pay Monthly site I set up, (discussed in the 'Hosted Website's chapter) all I had to do was click on a 'configuration' link and add my Google account number and the site did all the rest. Check with your provider to find out if they have this facility. Some will simply ask you to provide your Google Analytics Account number.

USING A DEVELOPER

If you have a development agency working on your site, they can insert the code into all the pages of your site, all you need to do is send them a copy of the code...

www.google.com/support/googleanalytics/bin/answer.py?answer=55603

Final Checklist

After all the hard work and elbow grease that has gone into creating this wonderful new website, it may come as an anti-climax when you first go live.

You have eaten, slept and breathed this site for who knows how long and now suddenly here it is, alive and kicking up in cyberspace. So first of all, take a deep breath and step back from it for a couple of days. Not only will this give you a well earned break, but it will also clear your head so you can review your site from a fresh perspective.

Ask friends, family and business colleagues to take a look and give their critique on your brand, your content and other aspects of the site. Also, if you have a community or membership site, you may want to ask them all to join up so you at least have a few members when you go live.

Road Test

It is essential to road test your site before you go live. There are a few things that you should do to ensure everything is ready to go:

- ❑ Check your branding throughout your site
- ❑ Check all fonts and colours match your brand
- ❑ Add your Favicon
- ❑ Check your content reflects your company image
- ❑ Follow your navigation map from different users' points of view to ensure if flows smoothly
- ❑ Test drive your buying process and buy something through your own shopping trolley
- ❑ Get a back up of your site
- ❑ Check email pop box and emails are working fine
- ❑ Make yourself visible with contact details
- ❑ Set up Google Analytics
- ❑ Submit to search engines
- ❑ Give yourself sufficient time to 'get going'
- ❑ Start special offers and competitions
- ❑ Get your PR release ready - see *Pimp My Site* for an in-depth PR study
- ❑ Start tweeting and sharing messages about your imminent go live date
- ❑ Check your URL with 'www' and no 'www' - both should work

❑ Ensure any error 404 pages contain a message from you – even though you will do everything you can to avoid errors, a few hitches may occur in the early days.

SOFT LAUNCH

Go for a 'soft launch' to ensure all bugs are erased and testing is complete before you start promoting the site. Teething problems will occur so take the time to get it right.

Checking The Checklist

There is so much we have covered in this book and I hope that you have made notes of your thoughts and actions in each section.

Now that you have a great set of checklists, you should go back to each one and remind yourself of things to do under each chapter, complete your research and formalise your notes.

Then check back one more time to ensure you haven't missed anything. All this detail is valuable and should ideally be stored in digital format.

Filling an Empty Restaurant

When your site goes live it is akin to a new restaurant opening. You have lovely new premises, content for Google's creepy crawlers to gobble up (explained in *Pimp My Site*) but no people to partake in the buffet. So what happens now?

When we were ready to go live with Remote Employment, we had no jobs on the site. How could we sell jobs to clients when we had no candidates to view the jobs? And how could we ask candidates to come to the site when there were no jobs? This is a classic chicken and egg situation – we had an 'empty restaurant'.

So we decided on a 'soft launch' to test the site with our first users. We offered free jobs to clients to get job content up on site and started PR campaigns in selected areas.

If you have this type of situation, you may also need to grow your content and members gradually and then, when your restaurant appears full, you can take off and launch yourself into full-on marketing campaigns.

Throw A Party

Now that you have almost finished this book, I want to congratulate you on sticking it out to the end. It is time for you to celebrate this fabulous new website. So, along with your PR release, throw a launch party. If you have products to show off and you have a bit of money to arrange a big bash, invite some of your local or regional media contacts along.

Depending on the type of site, and so many other factors, you could make a real hoo-ha event or a simple and stylish finger lunch or even an intimate coffee morning. Whatever you do, invite family and friends and work colleagues to fill the room and make your launch look the business, even if they pretend they are clients or customers. Talking of which, you will also invite potential site visitors to your celebration.

Most importantly, have fun, relish the moment and take pride in all the hard work you have done and the stunning new site you have created. Well done and congratulations!

Go Live

Now – press that big fat button that says: Go Live! Okay, so there's no actual button but your developer can do this for you. Or if you have a hosted site and you bought the domain yourself, you will need to get an 'A record', which is a set of numbers, and you will now point your domain to this Internet Protocol (IP) address.

WHAT'S AN IP ADDRESS?

Every device connected to the public internet is assigned a unique number known as an Internet Protocol (IP) address. An IP is a numerical label that is assigned to devices participating in a computer network that uses the Internet Protocol to find your website domain. Many hosting companies have scripts that automatically populate your IP and MX records, and all you need to do is point your domain name to their DNS servers. This is a much simpler concept, and all domain registration companies will allow it. It can take up to 48 hours for DNS servers to repopulate with the new data, but in our experience it's only been a few hours.

Inspire

I believe that passion and energy equals success. So don't be fazed by the fact that you're still small. Talk about your rate of growth, give people examples of your competitive edge and your competitive value. This often results in great conversations with potential partners, clients or advertisers.

Use your energy and eagerness to inspire others; it will bring a huge return on your investment as well as personal gratification. After the Remote Worker Awards winning ceremony we were inundated with finalists telling us how thrilled they were to be included in the Awards, even if they had not won. It set some people off on a mission to enter more awards, which they have gone on to win.

It is delightful to see their determination to be successful and all because something we did spurred them on.

When I talk at events and conferences, I love it when people come up to me afterwards and tell me how much they are inspired. Different things inspire different people. Some feel a sense of camaraderie because, in my small business, I have been in the same shoes and been challenged by the same situations. Sharing what these are and how I have overcome them may encourage someone to rush out and tackle their own struggle head on. Others may be moved by my determination to plough through the nightmare of pain and lack of sleep during my shoulder ordeal (long story!). Turning a negative into a positive brings people together in unusual ways.

Draw on your skills and expertise to inspire people you deal with you on a daily basis, even if it is only helping and guiding them in whatever sector you specialise. Use every opportunity to bestow confidence, motivate and stir people around you - it's a huge buzz!

Be Inspired

At the same time that you are inspiring others, be inspired by other websites and their trends, by people you meet and work with and by new innovations on the market. Keep thinking laterally and even insist on a monthly brainstorm with your management team, even if it is only two of you! And if you're on your own, brainstorm with yourself!

Why not? It will keep your inspirational juices flowing and this fluid is often the lifeblood of a new business.

Listen to people talking and ask questions about anything that sparks your attention. There are so many ways to earn revenue from a website so keep your options open, try different systems and maintain the solutions that work best for you. Go with the flow and remember that every website evolves over time.

Bees to Honey

Attract an audience like bees to honey. A business that is fresh and exciting attracts not only customers, client and thus orders, but also the media. They'll buzz around, all trying to get a taste of your nectar!

Give it freely because the more nectar you share, the more they'll come back for more. By this I mean, communicate your experiences, your generosity, your personality and talents. Build a simple media pack illustrating the important stats that would attract advertisers. Your Google Analytics will be a big help here.

Having an exceptional service or stunning product range will add to the excitement of knowing you and being around you. As your magnetic force grows in statue, so does your business and your bottom line.

The more you work at your website to make it a success, the more excited and empowered you will become. Allow your mind to float and drift freely at the end of each day. Think about what you have achieved so far and what you will achieve next. Day dream or sky dream by searching the endless blue to visualise the goals you set earlier in the book with clear visions and an intensity that makes you believe you will achieve them.

As Karen did, visualise your dream every day and constantly have an image in your mind of where you are going and how successful you will become. This will enrich your nectar and fuel your passion, which in turn will energise you and your business, turning it into a magnet and a beehive of success.

Summary

Today we experienced the final panic and pleasure of what could have been years, months, weeks or days of careful planning and implementation for your new site.

You have been back through all the notes in this book to ensure you haven't missed a trick and you are now ready to push that big fat green button which says: Go Live.

Checklist

❑ Add site to Google   ❑ Go Live Date
❑ Final Checklist   ❑ Go Live Launch
❑ Go Live Checklist

Afterword

Wait! Before you dash off, I wanted to remind you about all the cool things you should have learnt in this book.

Your successful completion of this book means that you are now ready to start the journey to becoming Google's Number One for your keywords. You should now feel pleased with yourself, happy, relieved, proud and revved up and rearing to go head on to market your new site.

Your next steps are to keep reading and learning more about online marketing and PR to keep your site optimised, marketed and publicised. If you enjoyed this journey with me, you may want to read my next book, *Pimp My Site*, which gives you hundreds of ways to optimise, promote, market and publicise your website.

Here's a reminder of the Key Points listed in this book:

- ❑ Research, brainstorm and plan your site - do what you know, where your experience and expertise lies
- ❑ Build your brand and keep it constant
- ❑ Plan your navigation map
- ❑ Decide if you are going to start with a simple blog
- ❑ Check out the different free websites
- ❑ Look into a pay monthly website
- ❑ Create a dialogue with your visitors with good content
- ❑ Make your content sticky and valuable to your audience so they keep coming back
- ❑ Interact with your audience by setting up a secure online shop
- ❑ Test everything before you go live

When you get through this list congratulate yourself and give yourself a great reward.

Finally, here's a list of the most important things you must do next to maintain a successful online presence:

- ❑ Use SEO Tools to ensure you get all the right keywords

- ❑ With your page plan, decide on your primary keywords to use in On Page Optimisation
- ❑ Ensure all the right Metadata is in place
- ❑ Start a link building campaign to create back links
- ❑ Sign up for Twitter, Facebook and LinkedIn
- ❑ Plan your marketing and PR campaigns and activities
- ❑ Write your launch press release and ongoing PR Strategy
- ❑ Try various PR Tools and media alerts
- ❑ Use email marketing as a highly cost effective promotional tool to connect with your audience

Lastly...

Thank you for reading my book and I hope you have enjoyed reading it as much as I enjoyed writing it! Please send me an email through my website contact page as I would like to show off your website and link the websites that have been created from this book.

I aim to have a special section for all the websites created from this book and I will feature them in my workshops, PR and courses. I would also like to invite you to attend any workshops or master class training courses on all the subjects in this book and my second book, *Pimp My Site*. I also work with small and large groups and I speak at events and seminars. Please browse www.paulawynne.com for more details.

Pimp My Site

If you enjoyed *Create a Successful Website*, don't miss out on my practical guide to optimising, promoting and marketing your website, also published by Lean Marketing Press.

Pimp My Site is a 'must have' online toolkit for Web savvy marketers.

Order your advanced copy now on Amazon and take advantage of my special 2nd book offer - see my website (www.paulawynne.com) for more details or to download a free sample chapter.

Glossary

BOUNCE: a term used when web visitors literally 'bounce' away from your website from the page that they landed on.

BOUNCE RATE: analytics track these bounces to inform you how many visitors you are losing.

BREADCRUMBS: a breadcrumb trail is a navigation aid that gives users a way to keep track of their locations within a busy site

CHARGEBACKS: these occur when buyers ask their credit card issuer to reverse a transaction that has already been approved.

CASCADING STYLE SHEETS: Cascading Style Sheets (CSS) is a Style Sheet Language used to describe the presentation, the look and formatting, such as the layout, colours and fonts, of a your web pages.

CMS: a CMS is software or an 'admin' area for managing your website content, thus known as a Content Management System.

CRM: Customer Relationship Management.

EXIT STRATEGY: is a way of exiting the business or company, either in an unsuitable situation or by forward planning.

FAVICON: a favicon is a small, 16x16 image that is shown inside the browser's location bar and bookmark menu when your site is called up. It is a good way to brand your site and increase its prominence in your visitor's bookmark menu.

GOOGLE ADSENSE: a flexible easy way to earn revenue online. You get paid for displaying Google ads on your site, where you can customise and target the ads to match your site's look and feel and track the results with reports.

GOOGLE ANALYTICS: this is the easiest way for you to track your traffic and analyse your website stats.

HTML: hypertext markup language - the code used to write web pages.

INTERNET MERCHANT ID: this can be obtained from acquiring merchant banks, not necessarily with your business bank account.

INTERNET PROTOCOL (IP): Every device connected to the public Internet is assigned a unique number known as an Internet Protocol (IP) address. An IP is a numerical label that is assigned to devices participating in a computer network that uses the

Internet Protocol to find your website domain.

MENTOR: is a wise and trusted counsellor or teacher or an influential sponsor or supporter.

NED: A Non-Executive Director (NED) is a member of the Board of Directors of a company who forms part of the executive management team, but may not be an employee of the company.

NICHE: a specialised and targeted industry sector.

POP BOX: is a nifty way to ensure that your email matches your company name.

PSP: An Internet Payment service Provider, or PSP, is when online payments are designated as 'cardholder not present' transactions and are considered by acquiring banks as 'higher risk' than cardholder present ones.

SEO (SEARCH ENGINE OPTIMISATION): is the process of improving ranking in search engine results.

SHOPPING CART: this is the software that collects all your purchases and calculates the total cost i.e. before you enter your card details

SITEMAP: enables you or your website to quickly show search engines which URLs (the individual address of each of your web pages) are available for crawling.

SMART GOALS: this means your goals are Specific, Measurable, Attainable, Realistic and Timely.

SM (SOCIAL MEDIA): is a group of easy to use web-based systems that allow you to engage with your audience.

SSL: a high level encryption SSL key to automatically encrypt confidential information.

SWOT: this analysis is a calculated way to plan and evaluate the Strengths, Weaknesses, Opportunities, and Threats involved in your online business.

URLS: the individual address of each of your web pages.

WIDGETS: a cool gadget that can be set up in various online platforms to create nifty tools to insert HTML code into your site.

WYSIWYG:-What You See Is What You Get - application for creating and editing websites.

XML: code readable by search engines

CPSIA information can be obtained at www.ICGtesting.com
Printed in the USA
LVOW081452110412

277163LV00003B/487/P